THE *glitterguru* ON
PHOTOSHOP
FROM CONCEPT TO *cool*

Suzette Troché-Stapp

800 East 96th Street, 3rd Floor, Indianapolis, Indiana 46240

An Imprint of Pearson Education

Boston • Indianapolis • London • Munich • New York • San Francisco

New Riders

The glitterguru on Photoshop: From Concept to Cool

International Standard Book Number: 0-7357-1133-X

Library of Congress Catalog Card Number: 2001087433

Printed in the United States of America

First printing: October 2003

08 07 06 05 04 03   7 6 5 4 3 2 1

Interpretation of the printing code: The rightmost double-digit number is the year of the book's printing; the rightmost single-digit number is the number of the book's printing. For example, the printing code 03-1 shows that the first printing of the book occurred in 2003.

Trademarks

Warning and Disclaimer

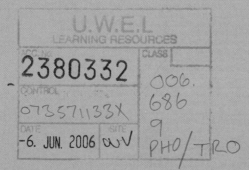

Associate Publisher

Stephanie Wall

Production Manager

Gina Kanouse

Acquisitions Editor

Elise Walter

Senior Development Editor

Jennifer Eberhardt

Project Editor

Michael Thurston

Copy Editor

Keith Cline

Indexer

Lisa Stumpf

Composition

Wil Cruz

Manufacturing Coordinator

Dan Uhrig

Cover Designer

Aren Howell

Marketing

Scott Cowlin
Tammy Detrich
Hannah Onstad Latham

Publicity Manager

Susan Nixon

Contributing Editor

Henry Pierce Stapp

❀

To the most extraordinary man I have ever met,
my husband, Henry Pierce Stapp IV

❀

Contents at a Glance

Table of Contents

About the Author

Suzette Troché-Stapp, a.k.a "the glitterguru," is one of the most sought-after photographers/digital artists today.

A pioneer in the field of digital art, she has been working with digital imaging since the early 1980s. In 1995 she co-founded the web-design firm Red Channel Interactive, which was soon widely acclaimed for its visually and technically groundbreaking work.

As an award-winning photographer and digital artist, her vast background has given her a wealth of experience in the intersection of art and technology. Her commercial images are as visually stunning as they are innovative, and she has built a client list that includes such well-recognized names as Hewlett-Packard, Bombshell Studio Make-Up, *Vibe Magazine*, *Entertainment Weekly*, Brooke Shields, Jenny McCarthy, Kathy Griffin, and others. Her images have been broadcast to millions on shows like "The View" and "The Late Late Show with Craig Kilborn."

In addition to her commercial work, this glitterguru is a Contributing Editor for *PEI Magazine*. Her monthly column, "Ask the Glitter Guru, Sage Advice for the Photoshop Fiend," gives advice based on real-world experience about what digital work for advertising entails. Suzette has also contributed to many other publications, including *Step by Step Electronic Design*, *Agosto Design* (Japan), *Micro Publishing News*, *Digital Imaging*, *Photographic Processing*, *What Digital Camera* (U.K.), *Digital Imaging* (U.K.), *Computer Foto* (Germany), and *Publish*.

Recognized throughout her industry, Suzette was recently named one of the "Top 40 Photoshop Experts" by Wacom, and was also awarded the 2001 "Guru Award" for excellence in Photoshop design by NAPP.

About the Technical Reviewers

These reviewers contributed their considerable hands-on expertise to the entire development process for *The glitterguru on Photoshop: From Concept to Cool*. As the book was being written, these dedicated professionals reviewed all the material for technical content, organization, and flow. Their feedback was critical to ensuring that *The glitterguru on Photoshop: From Concept to Cool* fits our readers' needs for the highest-quality technical information.

Seán Duggan is a photographer and digital artist who combines a traditional fine-art photographic background with extensive real-world experience in the field of digital imaging. He is a contributor to *Photoshop 7 Artistry: Mastering the Digital Image* (New Riders Publishing, 2002) and the second edition of *Real World Digital Photography* (Peachpit Press). He is an Adobe Certified Photoshop Expert and a member of the Photoshop beta test group. His Photoshop tutorial column can be seen regularly in *MacDesign* magazine, and he also writes articles on Photoshop and digital imaging for *PCPhoto*, *Outdoor Photographer*, and *Digital Photo Pro* magazines.

He is an instructor in the photography departments of the Academy of Art College in San Francisco and the University of California, Santa Cruz Extension in Silicon Valley, where he teaches regular classes on digital photography and digital imaging for photographers. Seán provides Photoshop and imaging consulting services for photographers and companies and also teaches annual workshops at the Palm Beach Photographic Workshops in Delray Beach, Florida, and the Lepp Institute of Digital Imaging in Los Osos, California. Sean's web site can be seen at *www.seanduggan.com*.

Wayne Palmer has had a passion for photography all his life. He has a degree in education from Bloomsburg State College, but his interest in photography kept him in the darkroom as much as the classroom. After graduation he worked for Guardian Photo Inc. in the marketing of photofinishing services on a national level for 13 years.

Wayne started his own business, Palmer Multimedia Imaging, in 1994, offering custom photographic, videographic, and digital photo-restoration services. He has worked with Photoshop since version 3 and previously with Aldus PhotoStyler.

A self-described AV nerd, Wayne enjoys sharing his knowledge of photography, digital imaging, and computers. He teaches Photoshop and digital photography at the Continuing Education Department of the Pennsylvania College of Technology, an affiliate of Penn State University.

Wayne was a contributor to *Photoshop Restoration & Retouching* (New Riders Publishing, 2001) by Katrin Eismann. He was a contributor as well as technical reviewer for the book's second edition

Acknowledgments

There is a multitude of people whose belief and talent have made this book a reality. First, and most importantly, I would like to thank the universe for my incredible family, especially my husband, Henry Stapp, for his undying and never-ending support of my artistic endeavors and for making my life a series of happy and joyous memories. Without him you would not be holding this book. He took my brain dump and turned it into a coherent series of words. I am blessed to have my soul mate who cheers me on and encourages me when I'm tired or overwhelmed, lets my crazy artistic whims turn our house inside out, and still after 12 years makes my heart skip a beat. I can't imagine how I was lucky enough to end up with the best guy on the planet (sorry ladies). On top of all of that, he is the co-creator of my most amazing and wondrous creation, my daughter, Merit Leighton, who fills my days with giggles and smiles. She is the reason why this book hit the market a year later than planned, and she has changed my life forever. Merit is incredibly beautiful inside and out, and her spirit is my guiding light. I am so truly blessed by the universe to have these two spectacular creatures in my world.

Another very important person who has been the president of my fan club since the day I was born is my mom, Brandy. She has given me undying support for everything I have always wanted to do. She bought me my first computer, a Commodore 64, and later on upgraded it to an Atari 512 (as in 512 kilobytes of RAM!), which is the machine I started doing digital imaging on many years ago. She supported me every turn and has always believed in me 100 percent. From buying me yarn to crochet a blanket (no Mom, I'm not going to finish the blanket) to microphones and jewelry findings—you name it—she made sure I had it. She sacrificed so that I could have the freedom to find what I had passion for, and I will forever be thankful for that sacrifice. Mom, I love you more than you could know; you are the best.

Next, I was blessed enough to have the universe bring me my friend, make-up artist to the stars, Cynthia Bachman—without whom this book wouldn't be nearly as pretty. My dear friend, she has done 90 percent of the make-up in this book and infused all of my projects with her fantastic, positive, creative energy. It wouldn't have been the same book without her, and it certainly wouldn't have been as fun. Along with being a brilliant artist, she is fantastic mom to her beautiful son, Mason, and an all-around awesome person...love ya!

I also want to thank many people at New Riders, especially Steve Weiss for believing in me enough to give me this opportunity. Steve, you are a wonderful person to work with, and your energy and enthusiasm has made this book what it is. Elise Walter, whom the universe sent down to crack the whip, I really needed you! Thanks for all of your hard work and input; you are awesome. And last, but certainly not least, Jennifer Eberhardt, my editor, and one of the people who got me into this whole mess. You are really great—your insights are fantastic and you wear glitter; what else can I say!

The Updegraft family: Sue, Gene, and their children, Alicia, Jacklin, Alexa, Garrett, and Landon. Thank you for giving up many weekends and after-noons to help me with photo shoots, grocery shopping, babysitting, and so on. Without your love and support, this book could never have happened. I love you with all of my heart.

Henry and Olivia Stapp, thanks for all of your support and the trips down to babysit Merit; your support has helped me make this book a reality.

Out West Studios, thank you so much for believing in me over the past few years. Your gracious gift of studio time to shoot my projects has been greatly appreciated. (Photographers, this is the best studio in Los Angeles; if you need to shoot in LA, go there!)

Judith Curtis, your costumes and styling have made my pictures better than I could have imagined; thanks for your artistic vision. You are truly a fantastic talent.

Jerome "JeRomeo" Andrew Terry, the sexiest hairdresser alive! Your talent shines through and we love having you in our creative circle. (Ladies, he's single!)

Terry Murphy, you gave me my first regular gig as a writer, and I am forever grateful! I miss talking to you once a month, but you're always in my thoughts.

Joan Sherwood and the staff of *PEI Magazine*, working for PEI is the best. Thanks for supporting my wacky style of advice and letting me be a part of this great magazine.

Terry Monahan, thanks for your belief in me as an author and for your donation of equipment to this project. Your advice, wisdom, and friendship mean the world to me.

Wence Chan, thanks for all of your insight and help. I better shoot the cover when you appear on *Time* magazine as businessman of the year!

Studio B, thanks to everyone for your help and support.

Models Susan Pari, Sasha, Elena Maddalo, Randi Jo, Lanisha Cole, Alexa Updegraft, Garrett Updegraft, Nina-Symone Williams, and Merit Leighton Stapp, thank you for all of your hard work on my stock shoots; your images are included here because of all of your hard work and talent.

Lynda Marrokal, for being my friend for as long as I can remember! For loaning me lights and studios and equipment when I first started years ago…and for generally being a great great great friend; I love ya!

Kym Williams and her daughter, Nina-Symone. Kym, thank you for giving birth to Merit's soul sister, the stunning Nina-Symone. You are a great friend and supporter. Kiss my baby for me…love you both to pieces.

I also want to thank the "Junatics." This is my group of online friends who all gave birth to beautiful babies during the month of June 2002. Your support and advice on everything from being pregnant to giving birth to being a WAHM has truly enriched my life…thanks to all of you.

Thank you to the following companies who have donated their products for this project: Alien Skin, Bombshell Studio Makeup, Chimera Lighting, Dyna-Lite, Flaming Pear, Fuji, and Procreate.

Tell Us What You Think

As the reader of this book, you are the most important critic and commentator. We value your opinion and want to know what we're doing right, what we could do better, what areas you'd like to see us publish in, and any other words of wisdom you're willing to pass our way.

As an editor for New Riders Publishing, I welcome your comments. You can fax, email, or write me directly to let me know what you did or didn't like about this book—as well as what we can do to make our books stronger. When you write, please be sure to include this book's title, ISBN, and author, as well as your name and phone or fax number. I will carefully review your comments and share them with the author and editors who worked on the book.

Please note that I cannot help you with technical problems related to the topic of this book, and that due to the high volume of email I receive, I might not be able to reply to every message.

Fax: 317-428-3280

Email: elise.walter@newriders.com

Mail: Elise Walter
          Acquisitions Editor
          New Riders Publishing
          800 East 96th Street
          3rd Floor
          Indianapolis, IN 46240 USA

Editors Elise, Michael, and Jennifer with their take on From Concept…

to Cool

"Stood Up" 2003

Welcome

I'd like to welcome you to our big, groovy, codependent-and-happy-about-it Photoshop family unit! I invite you to join us and hang out a while as I cook up some wild psychedelic pictures—you will not find this stuff in any other set of bound pages sitting on the shelf. This is your one chance to experience the glitter that only I can show you. You will not find fixed-up pics of Aunt June's family reunion picnic, but what you will find is real-life pictures from a wacky artist who wants to share her knowledge with you. I will speak my mind, share my wisdom, and give you my granny-like insights into this creative world in which I live and breathe.

Let's delve in and run amok.

In the Beginning...

Several years ago, a very wise man by the name of Steve Weiss stumbled across one of my articles in a magazine he was perusing. Steve thought I would be an ideal person to *review* books for New Riders Publishing; little did he know....

Jennifer Eberhardt, his fabulous associate, sent out to me a book to review and asked for my *honest* opinion. Trying to be as diplomatic as possible, I said, "Well, it's fine for a beginner but it doesn't really pertain to me as a professional." When she promptly informed me that the book *was* geared toward professionals, I thought to myself, "Ugh, open mouth insert foot!" Fortunately, Jennifer was intrigued rather than offended, and proceeded to ask me that fateful question: "What kind of book would you write?"

Prompted by that simple question, the floodgates opened, and I started fantasizing about the book that I wish I could have had when I started my career. The book you are holding in your hands represents the answer to Jennifer's question, and the realization of those fantasies.

Kathy Griffin for "The Late Late Show with Craig Kilborn"

Why Is This Book Different?

This book is not your typical Photoshop book. It doesn't focus on hardcore technical information—there are geniuses with names such as Ben, Bruce, and Bert* who write those books brilliantly. This book is here to help you stretch your brain cells into new and interesting shapes. It's designed to inspire you and make you want to be better than you thought you could be. To use a cooking analogy, this isn't a book of recipes—it's a book about how to become a chef.

So, What's in This Book?

Think of it as part career guide, part Photoshop theory book. The first chapters are a virtual brain dump of things I've learned over the years at the school of hard knocks—things you should know if you want to have a career as a digital artist or photographer. We'll talk about the mechanics of the business: working with art directors, storyboarding, estimating, and licensing, as well as the actual process of shooting the images. We'll also talk about marketing yourself, including things to do (and not do) when you're just getting started. Later, we'll delve into some Photoshop theory, and talk about the hows-and-whys of image compositing, retouching, and general digital mayhem. Relax, don't freak when I don't give you every click of every step I did. I want you to get the *idea* behind the clicks so that you can focus on the big picture.

Who Should Read This Book?

Beginners. If you are a beginner to the world of Photoshop and digital photography and you are embarking on a career in the field, the business chapters in this book are for you. There are so many things teachers or counselors *don't* tell you about working in the industry, and a lot of that is in the pages that follow: how to make money, how to present a portfolio,

---

* Ben Willmore, Bruce Fraser, and Bert Monroy

how to market yourself, how to work from start to finish on a concept. I will give you some of my tips and tricks in these areas so that you can start off with a bang.

Note that for the chapters that cover Photoshop techniques, I assume that you have a good grounding in the basics of Photoshop, so I don't cover the details of things such as how to use the selection or transform tools. For an introduction to these basic Photoshop techniques, I suggest either *Adobe Photoshop 7.0 Studio Techniques* (Adobe Press, 2002) by Ben Willmore or *Real World Adobe Photoshop 7* (Peachpit Press, 2002) by David Blatner and Bruce Fraser.

Intermediate and advanced users. There are lots of you out there who already use Photoshop as part of your daily professional work. If you would like some tips to help expand your career into advertising, or if you'd like to build on your knowledge and learn some advanced retouching techniques without having to wade through a lot of Ctrl+Alt stuff, this book will prove to be a valuable resource for you as well.

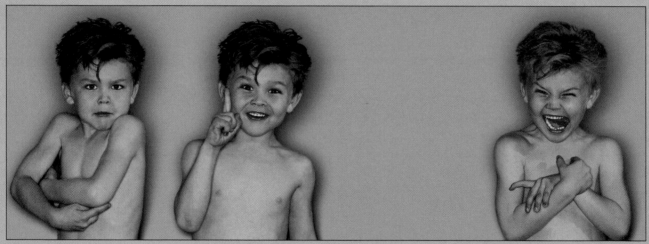

"Garrett Rex" 2001

Onward

Don't you hate it when you knock on the door to get in somewhere but someone says, "What's the password?" This, my friend, is truly an open book...no closed society with testosterone-filled rooms, or special secret handshakes for only the "special" people. Here, you are special; you *are* the "in" crowd.

So, that's my story and I'm stickin' to it. I know that if you lovingly caress these pages you will learn something. Now get up out of that chair...don't sit back and take the cold TV dinners served to us by guys in red ties and plain gray suits. Knowledge is freedom, and you should be free to pursue your wildest meanderings. Let your wings unfold as I pass the knowledge in glittery bursts of rainbow colors. Join us on this magic carpet ride...glitter, glitter, everywhere!

"Two Old Ladies" 2003

Chapter 1

Concept Creation

People, places, things; all shot in super-terrific, Hi-Fi color, in unexpected and exciting new ways. From the psychedelic caverns of thought or from a bright and shiny building on Park Avenue, concepts are given a green light. The happy, glittery toes of yours truly must visually satisfy the insatiable appetite of the viewing public. So let's begin the journey; get ready for a wacky trip that will move you from concept to cool.

Inspiration comes from an infinite variety of sources, and can strike at any time—while sitting half dazed in a lecture on color calibration, while stuck in traffic on the I5, or while scrubbing last night's lasagna off a green, plastic plate. As a Photoshop professional, your calling is to take these initial sparks of inspiration—both yours and those of your clients—and bring them into being as full-fledged creative works.

Where Do Images Come From?

In my career, most of the images I have created have come about in one of two ways. I can either come up with an idea from my twisted brain and shoot/image it, hoping someone will want it later, or I can be commissioned by a client or a client's agent to make their concept come to life. These two classes of work are referred to in the industry as *stock* and *assignment*, respectively.

Assignment Work

First let's dive into assignment work. Generally this type of work comes from ad agencies that may have clients from large, multinational corporations to small, mom-and-pop shops. The ad agency generally assigns an art director to a client's account, and the art director is responsible for coming up with concepts and storyboards for the client's campaigns.

Storyboards

Typically, the initial conceptual work on a campaign is done by the ad agency before photographers or digital artists are ever brought in. So, in most cases, you'll be presented with a completed storyboard and asked to realize it. The ad agency typically deals with the client at length, pitching concepts for possible campaigns using storyboards and quick mockups. After the client has picked the campaign they feel most comfortable with, the ad agency is responsible for bringing the approved concept to fruition. At this point, the photographers or digital artists are called upon; they are presented with a preset storyboard and given the job of bringing the image into being.

In rare cases, you'll be brought in earlier in the project and asked to help with the conception and storyboarding of the image. It is a high compliment to be brought in at the beginning of the storyboarding process—the art director is putting faith in you and your ability to contribute ideas that will help convey the client's message. Take advantage of these opportunities by

"Princess Merit" 2003

putting your creative energy to its full use, exploring possibilities and helping to create the vision of the campaign. If you can offer a new and unique viewpoint, based on your knowledge of digital imaging, clients will solicit your input as part of their creative process.

In some instances, you'll be called upon to create the storyboard yourself. You can use any method to create a storyboard, but the most commonly used method is to sketch out the idea freehand.

Occasionally, you will be given a storyboard with several elements at really impossible angles. In such cases, I always re-storyboard the concept. This enables me to give the art director an idea of what the "actual" image may look like. Clear communication is essential in these cases, so you want to be up front (while still being diplomatic) and let the client know whether there is something in the storyboard that you won't be able to pull off successfully.

Working with Art Directors

As a photographer or digital artist, the art director is the person you'll have the most contact with. An art director is the point person at the agency, the person who will be the go-between between you and the client, and the person who will provide you with the storyboard for the assignment's concept.

I have worked with my share of art directors, and just like anything else there are great ones and not-so-great ones. Your relationship with this person is vital to the outcome of the job, so you must establish excellent communication on an open and equal level. This is not easy and may sometimes even be impossible; nevertheless, it is critical. Here are some tips to help you establish and maintain good working relationships with art directors.

When starting out on an assignment, it is very important to question the art director to try to determine exactly what the art director's vision entails. Do not be intimidated in any way and do not be afraid to ask a lot of questions; good communication in both directions is a key to success.

In addition, you must be extremely clear in your own mind about what you yourself plan on delivering, when you'll deliver it, and how you plan on interpreting the art director's concept. Try to envision the concept as a finished image in your mind. I always know what my image will look like before I've even started. I see the finished image in my head and I know what I need to do to execute it before I sit down at my computer. Often in this artistic industry, clarity is difficult, but it is critical to the success of any image. Your clarity of vision will make it easier to communicate accurately and will help make the project a success.

What Do Art Directors Do?

What are an art director's responsibilities? Who better to ask than an art director. Here's what Wence Chan, a creative director, VP/art director at Grey Advertising in New York said about the responsibilities of an art director:

"Art directors get teamed up with a copywriter for starters. They brainstorm for an idea/concept according to strategy, and then they pitch that concept to the creative director and the client. Once the creative director and client approve the concept, rough comp layouts are created. When the comps are approved, then it's the art director's job to find someone to execute the image. The art director now works with an art buyer to search for photographers and artists. An art buyer's role is basically that of producer—that is, hire photographers, digital artists, schedule shoots, and get estimates.

"Once the shoot is scheduled, the art director goes to the shoot to direct the photographer and eat lots of free food; this is very important. The art director then returns with film or files and works with the digital artist to finish the image. After that process is complete, the art director sends the files to the graphics house to build the mechanicals, which include the image and any type that needs to be placed on the ad. When the mechanicals are completed, the traffic department sends them to the art director for approval (along with client approval). After final approval, the mechanicals are sent to the print production department, where the print production producer sends it out for match-prints. Match-prints return, and traffic takes it to the art director for approval again. Once approved, the ad is ready for the media."

"Aloha Nina" 2003

You can see what a big job art directors have, and why you are a key element in making the art director's client happy. So what's the best way to go about that?

What You Are Responsible For

As a photographer, it's important to dissect the storyboard you are presented and go over each element in detail. For the digital artist, it's important to involve yourself early on in this process. For projects that require lots of digital imaging, this is especially important, because there are things

"Sleeping Fairy" 2003

that you will think of and discover that the photographer may not realize, and vice versa. Photographers, I encourage you to bring in the digital artists you are working with as consultants on storyboards, shot breakdowns, and shoots. If the digital artists are responsible for creating the final composite, they will know what they need to create it. The process works more smoothly this way, and it saves everyone involved time and money.

As I've said before, it's very important to establish excellent communication with the art director. I have had my share of nightmares on *very* big jobs, when the concept was explained to me one way but was really intended to be something completely different. You really need to interview and question your art director. This goes for photographers and digital artists alike. Get as much artistic input as possible: color swatches, sample images, and detailed storyboards. Make written notes of important points on your copy of the storyboard and keep the notes in the job folder for future reference.

Talking with the Art Director

Here is a set of basic questions you can start with when first speaking about a project with an art director.

What Is the Deadline?

This is one of the most important pieces of information to have, but you will be stunned at how often your client will not know the answer to this question. Indeed, this question may never get answered if you are not persistent, because many projects are led by people who have trouble making decisions and just make things up as they go along. Obviously, the timeline you're working under affects everything on the project. This is especially true when it comes to estimating costs. After all, if the job is a rush, it may end up costing you 50 percent to 100 percent more in expenses and time, and this should be reflected in your estimate as rush fees. I have had art directors in the past claim that I was late delivering a job that had no deadline. So, be warned: If you don't have an agreed upon deadline, it's almost certain that the client will eventually make one up and then blame you for being late!

How Do You See This Concept Artistically?

Vision is an important question, but very difficult to get a solid answer about. Try to get the art director to explain a color palette, a mood, and, if possible, have the art director give some visual examples of what is intended. Take notes of your conversation, and summarize the key points on the storyboard you include with your final estimate. If the client has specific colors that they want you to use, have them send you sample Pantone swatches. If they should later come back and say, "Those aren't the colors I wanted," you'll be able to present them with the palette of swatches that they supplied you, to help refresh their memories. This also allows you to bill on a "change order" the extra time required to make any changes the client wants, because you can prove that the original work was done according to their specifications. Without a solid agreement on these kinds of details, the client may expect you to not charge them for changes because you did not complete the job "as specified."

Is This the Final Storyboard?

Again, you'd be surprised at how many times the answer to this is no, even though you're being asked to submit a bid on the project. It's absolutely imperative that every element in the storyboard given to you by the art director be as close to how they envision the final image as possible. This is key, especially in heavily composited final images. It's obviously also extremely important when bidding a project, because each element that's added or subtracted can change your bottom line. If they haven't got a solid storyboard together, draw your own (or have someone draw one up for you), and present it to the art director as your interpretation of the concept.

What Are the Final File Size Requirements?

This is very important, because working with very large files, or delivering several different size formats, can radically increase the amount of time you will have to spend working on an image. For instance, the client may need a really large file (for instance, 300MB flat). In layers, this image could be as large as 1GB. You must make sure that you have the resources (that is, a machine with more than 1GB of RAM) and the time necessary to work on a file this large. It may also change your costs; larger scans can cost more money and should be figured into your bid. The other variant that can make a difference is how many sizes they need. They may need a tabloid 11×14 inches as well as a billboard 20×15 feet. You may be able to use some of the

"Alien Boy" 2003

same elements, but really these are two different files that will need to be built. You need to explain to the client that this job really requires two completely different files to be composited, and that it will require extra time and cost.

Obviously each job will have its own set of individual questions that you will have to deal with. The previously listed questions should give you a good starting point. Remember to keep your dialog positive, and don't get upset when the inevitable changes or mix-ups occur. Working with other creative people in a collaborative effort can be a lot of fun, especially when everyone is on the same wavelength.

Honesty Is the Best Policy

A very important rule: *Always* tell the truth. I know it sounds silly and obvious, but you would be surprised how easy it is to begin saying what they *want* to hear rather than what they *should* be hearing. I mean, after all, you want this job, right? Make sure that it's not at the expense of your reputation. Always stick to your guns and know your parameters. My clients love me because when they ask for something and I tell them it will be done, they know it *will* be done. It is always there on time or early (they love it when you're early) and it's done properly. Don't let the client's demands, or your desire to get the job, detract from your ability to do on-time, quality work. Make sure that you can meet any deadlines that are laid out. After you have established a pattern of truthfulness, your clients will learn that they can always trust you.

Stock Work

Let's talk about stock for just a moment. Stock can be either something you've shot and imaged on your own or it can be an assignment project whose license has expired. (You'll learn more about licensing in Chapter 5, "The Business of Photography and Digital Imaging.")

Stock imagery is now where I make most of my income. It's a great way to work because you have total artistic freedom—there is no preset storyboard to follow. As always, however, with freedom comes risk, and you may wind up fronting the expenses to shoot an image that no one wants to buy. So, the responsibility is on you to create something that's marketable and to create images that consistently have your unique style imprinted on them. If you do this, you can eventually develop a regular clientele for your stock work. I have several regular clients who come to me for my imagery, and I often shoot with them specifically in mind. Despite this ongoing relationship, because I'm producing stock work rather than assignment work, I still have complete creative control.

Fees and Expenses

Chapter 5 covers the money aspects, estimating, and licensing in detail, so for now let me just mention the things that distinguish assignment work from stock work in this respect.

On an assignment job, the ad agency pays for several things. Here is a breakdown:

❖ **Expenses.** When doing a bid on assignment work, you must first assess the storyboard given to you by the agency. Break down the image and determine how much this job will cost. Keep in mind that production costs for any given image can potentially cover a huge range, depending on the production value expected by the customer.

A high-production-value assignment might be budgeted to include a photo shoot with wardrobe, makeup, supermodels, travel, and custom-built sets. The same concept could be executed, with a much smaller budget, perhaps using a combination of existing stock photos and a bare-bones photo shoot.

The budget the customer has allocated for the project determines what kind of production value you can deliver, so it becomes a critical part of your estimating equation. Try to get as much of this information out of the art director as you can so that your estimate doesn't come in too high or too low.

❖ **Artistic fees.** On the photography side, fees are set according to the license you negotiate with your client. Chapter 5 discusses licensing in more detail; so for now, just know that the license fee is based on what kind of usage your client wants to make of the image.

On the digital imaging side, fees are billed as part of the production cost of the image and are calculated on an hourly basis. When you're estimating a project, you should include a ballpark estimate of how many billable hours of digital imaging work are required. Base this estimate on your breakdown of the storyboard the art director gives you. Again, according to your experience, per-hour fees range from $150 to $1,000.

In contrast to assignment photography, where the client pays the expenses, license fee, and creative fees, with stock you generally pay the expenses out of your own pocket, hoping to license the image later.

On rare occasions, an agency will ask you to create an image on "spec." What this usually means is that they will pay the expenses but no fees or licensing until the image is sold.

Communication is the key factor in being able to come to the end of the job and have the client and art director be happy campers. Only then can you feel confident that you've done your job correctly, and that you'll keep them coming back for more. These good relationships based on trust can make your career. Clients will return over and over again to people they know are easy to work with and consistently deliver quality work on time. Be one of these people and your career will flourish.

Where We Are

So, the concept has been hatched, and you've been given the storyboard. You've asked all the right questions of the art director, and have hopefully established a clear and common vision with them of what you are trying to achieve. Now comes the fun part, actually creating the image. Let's forge ahead and start by looking into some of the mechanics of shooting the images you're going to need for your final product.

"Meadow Fairy" 2003

Chapter 2

Preproduction

Fire up the lights, grab a camera, and spring into action. Putting it all together and making the concept a reality is the job at hand. How? Let me take you step by step down the yellow brick road and over the rainbow to my little Hollywood—where I turn pixels into little frozen films. Get ready, and quiet on the set.

All the photography shown in this book is digital. All the images were shot on either the Fuji S1 or S2, and I absolutely love my cameras! Digital is the greatest thing to ever happen to my work, so much so that I could never go back to film. I think the main reason why I love this medium so much is that I'm addicted to the instant gratification. Even when I shot film in the olden days, I would often use Polapan, an instant 35mm slide film. I loved it because I knew in 3 minutes whether I got the shot.

Obviously, I'm quite comfortable in the digital world. In my experience, it makes shooting much less stressful. I feel secure knowing that my job is done, exposed correctly, and saved on to my hard drive at the end of the day. It makes for a happy crew, too. The make-up and hair people love it because they are looking at the actual image on my computer screen while I shoot. This instant feedback gives them the luxury of perfecting their work before the shot is "in the can." Art directors also love digital because they don't have to wait until the next day to view and edit film. The shots are edited on the same day, which allows me to get to work right away on the imaging part of the job. It's great for tight deadlines and eliminates costly scans, which helps keep your prices down.

I'm not going to go into my whole workflow and system setup; there are plenty of other books that discuss these types of issues. My goal is to offer a suggestion that you hesitant film photographers go out and try digital.

I think that, artistically, digital photography enables you to be more creative, because you can try a variety of things quickly without having to wait for film to develop to see the results. Moreover, you see your lighting on the actual final shot, not on a Polaroid, which often doesn't match in color or saturation. In my experience, many times Polaroids on a job appeared to be fantastic, but the actual film fell a little flat because of disappointing color rendering.

For anyone starting out in this business and reading this book, think about starting out with digital. I really think that someday film will be for fine art only and the mainstream of photography for advertising will be digitally based.

Getting the Concept in the Can

This chapter walks you through the production of one of my stock shoots, covering all the things to keep in mind when progressing from concept to photograph. This chapter covers breaking down a storyboard, hiring your team, casting, props, preproduction, and more. If you ever wanted to know how to put together a top-quality shoot, keep reading.

Creating a Shot List

You may be asking yourself, "So I got the job...now what?" The first thing I do after getting an assignment is to break down the storyboard the art director has given me and come up with a list of elements needed to create the final image.

The example image for this chapter is "Butterfly Fairy." I created this image for my stock portfolio to be presented to a couple of my regular stock photo clients. I wanted to do a fairy image that was a little bit sultry and dark but beautiful at the same time. The concept had come to me in my dreams, which happens to me fairly often: The dark fairy girl with blowing hair will be surrounded by butterflies. She will be wearing a silver necklace with a large stone set in it, and an image of a forest will be inserted in place of the stone as a postproduction step. Major visual features of the shot will include *a lot* of blowing hair, as well as the butterflies floating throughout.

Analyzing the image, you can create a quick list of the various elements you need to shoot. This is called a *shot list*. Shot lists are crucial for pulling together complicated imagery. Shot lists also help your crew know what they have to accomplish for any given project and help keep you on time and on track. From the storyboard, you can see that the major elements include the model, the butterflies, blowing hair, and the necklace.

Butterflies   Model

Hair   Necklace

1   The storyboard for the "Butterfly Fairy" image, with the main elements called out.

The following shot list identifies what needs to be shot and in what order:
Shot List

1. Model with hair blowing
   ❀ Extra frames of model with hair blowing
2. Butterflies
   ❀ Many different angles of butterflies
3. Location image of forest to insert into necklace

Gathering Your Team

After determining the requisite things to shoot, what's the best way to go about it? First you must gather the team you need to help you create the image. For a shoot such as this, a typical team would include a make-up artist, a hairdresser, a stylist for wardrobe and props, and an assistant to help with general production tasks. If you're thinking, "Gee that sounds like a lot of people," you're right. However, having the right team in place really lets you focus on getting the image right, instead of running around like a crazy jack-of-all-trades. I know that not all of you have the resources to hire an entire crew; I suggest getting together and meeting with as many people as possible who specialize in these different areas. You may find some excellent people that you just hit it off with, and they may be willing to do tests (unpaid work), or perhaps lower their rate, because they like your work and want to be a part of it. I have found that many artists whom I meet have a passion for creating images and want to work. So be creative and generate a collective of artists whom you can rely on.

In my opinion, I am only as good as the people I'm working with. Thank goodness they rock! I'm really fortunate to have great people I work with on a regular basis whom I can rely heavily on for support and inspiration. My crew for this shoot included make-up designer Cynthia Bachman, Jerome Andrew Terry for hair, and Susan Updegraft as all-around great assistant. Normally I would have a stylist as well. In this case, however, because the shot doesn't require any costumes or clothing, I didn't need a wardrobe person. Looking at everyone's calendars, we decided to schedule the shoot for January 26.

Photo shoot crews are often not emphasized enough, but always remember that the people who work with you can make you look good or bad. Always respect them, feed them, and listen to their valuable input! A lot of times I talk over my shots with various members of my crew. Their observations make me think harder and make the final outcome that much better. You are paying them for their creative input; they are a big part of the vibe that you want to create in your shoot atmosphere and in the images that shoot produces. I love my crew, and I love to shoot because we have a blast. They are my working family, and I try to treat them as such.

Casting a Model

After you have your team in place, the next step is to cast a model. I do a lot of stock photography, so casting is very important. In an assignment job, the art director is usually at the casting and works with you to pick the model after looking at the test shots. In a stock shot, you pick the model yourself, and having the right person in the shot can make all the difference as to whether the image sells. Of course, casting is very subjective, so it's hard for me to say what the "right" person is in general terms. Modeling is about a lot more than being pretty—it's basically a form of acting. A good model shows up with a professional attitude and gracefully puts up with long hours, hot lights, endless make-up and hair retouches, pinching clothes, tight shoes, and contorted positions. They need to be able to bring their own emotional focus and intensity to your shot, working with you to help achieve your creative vision. I usually try to pick seasoned models who can give me the look or attitude I'm seeking. Often it may be an image of them in their portfolio or on their *Zed card* that makes me go "ahhh, that's it!" Go with your gut instinct. You may not score every time, but your instincts will get better and better with each and every casting.

Zed cards (also called comp cards) are a model's equivalent of a mini-resumé. They are generally two-sided cards about 5×7 inches in size, with an assortment of shots of the model, usually including a headshot, full-body shot, and perhaps any shots from campaigns the model has done. Zed cards are a standard in the industry, and almost any professional model will have one. If someone sends you an 8×11 headshot, this is usually a clue that they are more of an actor, something to consider when looking for a seasoned model.

The casting process starts when you place an ad with a local casting service. These usually are free of charge to professional photographers offering paying assignments. In the Los Angeles area, I use both Photographer Express and Breakdown Services (*www.breakdownservices.com*). If you're not in LA, I suggest contacting your local talent agencies and creating relationships with them. Tell them that you will need models throughout the year and perhaps set up an appointment to show them your work.

To place a casting call, you just call the agency or casting service and tell them what you're looking for. For example, an ad may read, "Looking for females 18–23, model types, all ethnicities." You should also specify what the shoot is for and how much it's paying. For example: "For stock photo shoot, buyout $500, 8 hours plus 1-hour lunch, including agency." For this particular shoot, I wanted a broad range of talent. I didn't have an absolute "type" in mind. Because of this, I left the ad description quite open so that I would have myriad choices sent to me.

For a stock shoot, you must have a "buy-out" release from the model. This kind of model release gives you the flexibility to use the image in any way you want, without having to compensate the model for its future uses. It's imperative to have this control, because you have no idea where the image will end up or how it will be used. In fact, you don't even know whether the image will sell at all. This uncertainty is the reason why stock pays the model a fixed fee. The agency charges you a one-time fee and gets its money up front—you take the risk of putting the money out for the shoot and perhaps not being able to sell the image. On an assignment job for an ad campaign, the negotiation with the model's agency can be a little trickier. Often the modeling agency won't give you a buy-out because the usage of the image is known ahead of time, and the agency will want the model to be paid according to the usage. Most of the time, you negotiate a release for the model that is the same as your license. The fee for the model depends on where the image is being used, what company is using it, and for how long—very similar to your how your licensing is determined. If you later want to use the same image for another purpose, you have to renegotiate with the model's agency for another fee.

After I place my ad, I usually receive a ton of headshots and Zed cards within a few days. As they come in, I go through them and pick out my top choices. Then, I either have the models' agencies send me their portfolios or, if time permits, I have all the top choices come in for a casting day. The purpose of the casting day is to take some test shots of the leading candidates, meet them, and see how they come across on camera. There are obviously some costs associated with having an actual casting day. You need a fairly central location to have the models come to, and you will probably need some assistance in dealing with the logistics of getting all the models in and out smoothly. I usually have the models sign in on a numbered sign-in sheet. As they arrive, they are asked to fill out an information sheet. This sheet will then have their number for the day written on it. Their number on the sign-in sheet correlates with the number that is written on the info sheet. For the first shot of every model, I have them hold up this sheet; that way, I don't mix up names and I know who's who after a long day of casting (see Image 2). This information sheet has their vital statistics, name, agency, height, weight, dress size, shoe size, bust, waist and hip measurement, and a place for notes if they have a comment they want to add. I also always ask on the sheet whether they are available on the day I have chosen to shoot. Sometimes the agency doesn't have time to ask each and every model they send you, so it's a good idea to double-check.

Some agencies won't send you anything, but many others will flood you with responses to your ad. Get ready for a lot of mail! Be sure to always add "including agency" when specifying fees in your ads. Otherwise, the agency will tack on its fee—typically 20 percent—on top of the fee you specify.

Casting is hard work, but well worth the effort. You may literally have to go through hundreds of pictures to find a few models you will even consider. Unfortunately, some agencies blast out a model's card in response to any ad, even if only the gender matches! Because of the volume of work that can be involved, many photographers work through casting agents. These casting agents can do much of the initial filtering work for you, sorting through all the photos of people who are clearly not what you're looking for. I prefer to do all the casting work myself, however, because only I know exactly what I'm looking for and exactly what will and won't work.

Whenever I hold a casting day, I have a light setup so that I can snap one or two pictures of each model myself. This helps me get a feel for how they move and work in front of the camera. After shooting for a while, you'll know the good models by their professionalism and their ability to work in front of the lens.

The advance work of a casting day makes the actual shoot a bit easier, because you will already have some shooting experience, albeit brief, with the model. Sometimes, however, as in the case of the "Butterfly Fairy" image for this chapter, there isn't time to do a casting day, and you will have to pick a model based on Zed cards and portfolios. In this particular production, I had to schedule the shoot for a day that all of my A-list crew would be present, but that meant that there wasn't time for a separate casting day. Rescheduling would have meant putting off the project for several months. In this case, my crew's schedules came first, and I decided to cast based on the Zed cards alone.

2   Shot from casting day showing a model with an information sheet.

Props

At this point we've dissected our storyboard and created a shot list, we have our crew in place, and the shoot is scheduled. Now we need to get together any necessary props. If the shoot requires hard-to-find, elaborate, or custom-built props, you may need to bring in a stylist to help pull everything together. On this shoot, however, my assistant and I procured the props because there weren't many of them and I knew exactly what I was looking for.

Props can come from just about any kind of place, from prop houses and costume-rental stores, to a friend's living room. In this case, in addition to the normal schedule for getting props together, we added extra time to find a necklace that fit in with the style of the shoot and had enough space to fit the forest scene within it.

Storyboards to Crew

At the same time that you start looking for props, it's a good idea to send out the storyboard to the crew and, if possible, the model. This helps everyone to get on the same channel, so that everyone shows up with a common vision; it also gives them time to get their creative juices flowing in advance of the shoot.

Monday	Tuesday	Wednesday	Thursday	Friday	Sat/Sun
January 13	14 Send out Casting Call	15 Find Butterfly, necklace & tube top	16 Email Storyboards to crew	17 Go through castings and choose model	18
					19
20	21 Hire Model- Shoot landscape for necklace.	22 Order catering	23 Send out map to studio location with times and contact info	24	25 Pre-Light prep for shoot
					26 Photo Shoot

3 The calendar for the "Butterfly Fairy" photo shoot.

Other Preproduction

As you can see from the calendar, I put out my casting notice on Tuesday, January 14. I was already getting packages early the next morning, and immediately began searching through the piles for the perfect model. I came across Sasha's card quite quickly and saw that she was with OTTO models, with whom I have worked in the past. Sasha was on the top of my list from day one; she had an unusual look and her card showed that she had done some excellent work.

At the same time, I began to design the lighting setup. I usually start with at least a basic diagram and then experiment a little to make it all work just perfectly. (The next section discusses lighting in more detail.) Suffice it to say that you want to use the time before the shoot to think through your lighting setup. Get your lighting diagrammed out, make sure you have all the equipment you need ready, and rent any special pieces you need for the setup you have in mind. My assistant, Susan, and I spent the rest of the week looking for props. I happened to come across the perfect butterflies by chance on the Christmas clearance table of a local home improvement store, which left us with only the necklace to find. In the end, we bought six different necklaces because we knew we wouldn't be able to decide which one was right until we saw it on the model in front of the camera.

On assignment work, I always compile a folder for each person on the crew as well as for the art director. In the folder, I include the following:

A printout of the storyboard

A shoot calendar showing preproduction through final delivery of the image(s)

Contact information, including the cell, fax, and email of all crew members

Location maps

Scratch paper

A pen

Because assignment shots often involve a lot of people, these folders give everyone involved the critical information they need to communicate with each other all the way through preproduction and shooting.

Over the weekend, I continued to go through the models' cards, but I kept going back to Sasha. I decided she was perfect, and on Monday gave the agency a call to book her for January 26. It occurred to me that Sasha's hands might be seen, so when I hired her I told the agency I would give her a $20 allowance for a manicure, and asked that she get her nails done in a dark burgundy color that would fit the image.

The only thing that wasn't going to be shot on January 26 was the image to go inside the necklace medallion. The concept called for a landscape with trees and perhaps water. On January 21, I made a trip out to a local arboretum and got a great landscape shot for the necklace. In this particular case, there were no lighting issues to take into consideration because the image in the medallion was supposed to represent the girl's homeland. I wanted a sense of peeking into another world and was hoping to create that with a totally different look within the medallion.

A couple of important things were still left to do. Studio location maps with times and important phone numbers were sent out, either by fax or email, so everyone knew when and where to be for the shoot. Catering was arranged to have lunch and snacks available during the day. This is *very* important. Feed your crew well; they will be very happy that you did, and brains function better on a happy tummy.

You will find along the way that certain agencies really have a better caliber of talent. Build a rapport with these people. After establishing a good working relationship, you can just call them and tell them what you are looking for. Sometimes you won't even have to do an open casting call.

Lighting Setup and Test Shots

The morning of January 25, we began to set up the lighting for the shoot. I begin the lighting process by setting up the studio following a basic lighting diagram I create for the image. Although things may change as the shoot unfolds, the initial lighting diagram provides a starting point. Next, I get a test subject in front of the lighting setup for some test shots. The idea of the lighting tests is to get the lighting 90 percent done, so that when the model shows up it's just about working with her to get the perfect shot, and not about deciding how you're going to light the image.

I knew the make-up for this shot would have a lot of glitter, and I wanted to make sure the lighting enhanced it. So, as a test subject, I borrowed my niece and got her covered with glitter (lucky girl), and then put her in front of the camera for a couple of hours and began to experiment (see Image 4).

On every project, start a job folder. This is particularly important for assignment work, which requires you to manage lots of paperwork. Start the job folder when you bid a project and store your receipts, invoices, and copies of any pertinent communications in this folder. Also, I like to have it by the phone when talking to a client so that I can use it to record notes. It's nice because it keeps everything is in one place.

4　Initial lighting diagram for the "Butterfly Fairy" shoot.

Lighting is one of the most important things to try to master.
Although there are plenty of books on photographic lighting out there, in the end it's critical
to have your own equipment to learn and experiment with. Dyna-Lites (www.dynalite.com) are my personal
favorites, because they are highly efficient and compact. (As I always say, "Dynas are a girl's best friend.")

If you don't have your own equipment, find someone who might let you borrow their equipment. Perhaps even rent a small setup for a weekend and experiment with your family or friends. Even if you can only get your hands on one old can light and a reflector card, you can do a lot with these simple items. A great way to learn is to try and copy lighting you see in fashion and advertising. First try to determine what kind of lighting setup was used by looking at the catch lights in the model's eyes. This is often an excellent way to analyze an image's lighting setup. Pick a shot that looks good to you, and then try and get the same lighting effect yourself.

You can never be good enough at lighting—you'll always be learning more. With practice, however, you'll develop an eye for lighting and be able to tell almost immediately what kind of setup was used to create an image. This knowledge will serve you well. It will enable you to take an image you are visualizing and quickly lay out the lighting setup you need to realize your vision.

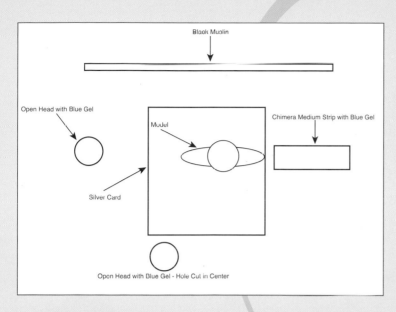

Black Muslin

Open Head with Blue Gel

Model

Chimera Medium Strip with Blue Gel

Silver Card

Open Head with Blue Gel - Hole Cut in Center

5 Lighting test, showing the original lighting as diagrammed.

Dynalite 2040 Head
with Chimera small strip

Dynalite 2040 Head with
Chimera medium strip with blue gel

Dynalite 4040
Open Head with amber gel

Dynalite 4040 Head with Chimera x-small
softbox—blue gel with a hole cut in the middle

6 The final lighting setup used for the shot.

7　An unretouched image of a shot using the final lighting setup.

By the time the test shots were done, I ended up changing a few things from the initial setup (see Image 6). I kept the open head on the left, but switched to an amber gel. On top I added a small strip for an extra light on the hair. On the right I stayed with the original medium strip with the blue gel, and on my main light I just added an extra small softbox, to diffuse the light, and a blue gel with a large hole cut in the middle on the inside of the box. This was the setup used for the actual shoot the next day.

As you can see from Image 7, the lighting setup helped the image capture the right mood for the dark fairy concept. Having a good place to start from in Photoshop is key; I try to do as much as I can in camera and work from there. Lighting was a crucial element in making this image moody and sultry, and the effect probably could not have been created in Photoshop as effectively. At this point, I was thrilled with the raw material I was going to get to play with later.

The Shoot

Call time the morning of the shoot was 11 a.m. To make the most out of everyone's time and effort, we planned to do two different shots in one day. Whenever I do a two-shot day, I always have one shot with light make-up and build up to the second shot with heavier make-up. Put your most important shot second if possible, that way everyone has a chance to work with each other and get into a groove. It's very beneficial because I get an idea of what the model's best angle is and I have a feel for how the model moves and reacts.

We ended up taking about 300 shots of various poses for the "Butterfly Fairy." In this case, I was really trying to get the model to evoke a certain feeling. It was extremely important that the feeling she exuded went with what would be created around her. The model needed to do something similar to what actors do when working with a blue screen. They do not have the luxury of seeing the amazing set they will be placed into later. That's why, in the case of the "Butterfly Fairy," I gave Sasha the story behind the image. I told her that her fairy character lived in the world contained in her pendant and the butterflies were like her children. She was to beckon them to come from her land, which lies within her pendant. Sasha was fantastic. She really understood the concept and gave me exactly what I needed. Remember, the model is there against a plain backdrop. To really make images come together, models must "be" in the world that you create. It's your job to help put them there within their own minds. Think of yourself as a director with only one frame in which to tell your story.

Lighting is extremely important in creating a composited image because, if you want things to meld together in the image, the light must hit each object in the same way. Make sure when you go to create a composited image that you have everything you need to shoot for that final photograph so that the lighting conditions can remain unchanged throughout the shoot. I generally shoot the model first because this is when most of the lighting adjustments are made.

The day went very quickly. After finishing the main shot, we grabbed a lot of extra frames of Sasha's hair blowing. We wrapped with the main portion of the shoot by 5:30 p.m., which made it a relatively short day for most of the team. We left the lighting setup in place so that we could photograph the butterflies under the same light conditions as the model.

To get the butterfly elements, I had my assistant hold the butterflies at various angles in slightly different parts of the set: some closer to the amber gel, some closer to the blue gel, some closer to the main light, and others closer to the background.

Having a variety of lighting angles on your elements like this helps later when you are picking which ones to put where. The elements look like they were actually part of the original shot because the light is hitting them correctly. You could, of course, adjust for this in Photoshop, but it's just

Always snap a shot of your set when you are finished just for the record books. You would be surprised how many times an art director will come and ask for that exact lighting from your portfolio. Make it easy on yourself by taking that one extra frame so that you can re-create it at the drop of a hat.

easier to shoot it correctly in the first place. We photographed the butterflies for about 45 minutes and finished the day around 6:30 p.m., just in time for dinner.

We now had all the elements needed to create the "Butterfly Fairy" image. (Chapter 6, "Beauty Retouching," covers some of the retouching techniques used to create the final image.)

Postproduction Imaging

When shooting an image for stock or assignment, it's important to think about the dimensions of the final image. When this image is complete, it would be a good size for a double-page magazine ad. However, what if the buyer decides that he needs a one-page tabloid with room on the left for type as well?

Well, a couple of things can make your life easier. One is to photograph the black background just by itself (just to have around to add extra space on the left). You might say, "It's just black," but there are many different colored pixels that make up that particular black background, and it's easier to just paste in a piece from the background file than it is to try to match it later. Also, photograph the model vertically as well as horizontally. It will give you more options to work with if you have more of her body to image with.

You can see from Image 8 how having more shoulder would make creating a single-page ad quite a bit easier. It may require literally redoing the image, but many times clients are willing to pay for this because they don't need to put out money for an extra shoot. These extra shots take only a few seconds, but can save you time and give you more flexibility later if you need to modify the format of the shot.

Enter the Art Director

On this particular image, I was shooting for my stock portfolio. If this job had been an assignment for a specific client, however, I would have done some things differently because I would have been working with an art director.

8 Vertical shot taken for future format flexibility.

Creative Collaboration

Although art directors have the final say over everything, keep in mind that you have been hired for *your* creative abilities—your input is vital. I always like to give art directors a selection of options on some of the variable parts of an image. This is really a key factor in working with a person in this position—give the art directors options so that they feel like there is a place for their creative input. This also encourages a good, two-way creative communication process and helps keep everyone working on the same track.

Working with an art director would have forced some specific changes in how the two weeks of preproduction were spent, because art directors sign off on several critical steps of this process. Selection of the team requires the art director's sign off, so an initial list of recommendations would be made as to whom you felt the right crew members would be. You submit such a list for the art director's approval. As stated previously, the art director would also be given several options for each of the main elements (butterflies, necklace, and image for the necklace). Several different versions of each would be photographed and presented a week or two before the day of the shoot for the art director to select.

When it comes to casting, again the art director gets the final word. Therefore, send an edited version of the casting to the art director with your top picks separated out.

With a make-up—such as this one, which is so important to the image— preproduction drawings would be submitted to the art director for approval. On the day of the shoot, the art director would have input over the make-up and would be asked to sign off on it as well.

As each of these items is approved, I keep a paper trail. I keep hard copies of any faxes and printouts of all emails and add them to the job folder. That way, at the shoot, I can retrieve any of these documents with ease, if necessary.

Sometimes on assignment work your art director is in a different city. When I worked with Wence Chan at Grey Advertising on a project a few years back, for instance, we communicated via phone or email almost every day during the project. He was based in New York, and I am in LA, but we both have fast net connections. So, on the day of the shoot I sent proofs via email for his approval while the shoot was happening. This worked out great; even though separated by the whole country, his input was felt every step of the way.

Getting Sign Off

Sign off is *very* important. I have often had the experience of an art director saying, "I never approved those colors," when he in fact did in front of my entire crew. Unfortunately it's a lot harder to argue your point than just to point out a memo that the art director sent you. You need more than witnesses to back up your side of the story; you need documentation to CYA! That way there is never a question of what you were told to do, and when you were told to do it.

This also holds true for the digital imaging portion of the job. Every time you send the client a revision of what you're working on, get the changes in writing. Send a "change order" memo, which is just a form with a description of the work you will be doing. Email communication provides this "written" record without any additional steps.

At the Shoot

At the shoot, try to keep the atmosphere professional but not necessarily stuffy or uptight. Make sure the art director is treated with the respect deserved. If you're not able to personally see to the art director's needs, make sure that someone is (making sure they've got their coffee and Danish and so on). On set, ask for the art director's input as to lighting, the angle, everything! Art directors have a big influence on the success of your project, so it's important to have them feel involved as well as comfortable and happy. My shoots are always on the laid-back side, but you still know that a lot of work is being done despite the casual style. I think it's something you acquire through the years: a sort of shoot style. If your preproduction is done properly, most of the time your shooting should be stress free. You want the art director to come away with a pleasant, memorable, and creatively fulfilling experience.

Where We Are

We've prepared, hired crew, cast a model, set our lighting, and finally produced our raw images. The shoot is a wrap, and the shots are in the can. We are now at about the 50 percent point in the production of this image. Now how do we put it all together? The next chapter examines what to do at this stage of the game. I walk you through a few scenarios that will help you understand the thought process behind "how" I create an image.

Chapter 3

Creating the Image

Curtains up! What part will we act out in this play? Set builder? Astronaut? You have a front-row ticket, and the show's about to start. So sit down in your velvet seat, as little girls and aliens take center stage.

So you got the job, broke down the storyboard, and then went out and shot the elements—now you need to put the pieces together into a coherent whole. I'll go into details on specific retouching tips and techniques in later chapters; but first, I'm going to cover the overall creative process for creating the image. This obviously involves picking the right shots and then compositing them so that they blend together seamlessly; it also involves making sure that you adhere to the underlying artistic vision throughout the process.

Every image is different, so there are no absolute rules here. With this in mind, however, I'm going to discuss two images, detailing the process behind each one. This will hopefully provide some food for thought and help you think about how to approach creating an image.

We begin with an image called "Alexa." I am using this as a starting point because it's not too complicated. It's simple in design and construction, so you'll be able to understand the basic theory I'm going to convey.

Preparation

The story of this shot is that of a little girl who gets bored and decides to play dress up in Mom and Dad's closet. She picks up Dad's shirt, Mom's shoes and purse, and so on. Then she pretends to be a fashion model. The twist I wanted to achieve was to create a more sophisticated image than just that of a child playing. I wanted to extract the archetype of the underlying concept of the child, and contrast this in a formalized setting, using only the basic elements of the scene. The goal was to introduce a stark simplicity to the image, creating a subtle visual dissonance between a child at play and the rigid postures and settings she is forced to exist within.

1 "Alexa"

As I imagined this, the words *innocence*, *realism*, and *military* came to mind. I'll talk more about this later, but for now I'll mention that I try to think of words to focus on while I'm working. The words help serve as guideposts for the concepts that I'm trying to get the image to evoke. Having the right frame of mind when you start is very important. Knowing what your goal is, not just technically, but in terms of the underlying messages the image will convey, makes a world of difference.

Armed with this concept and a hard disk full of freshly shot images, I moved on to the first step of the compositing process: picking the actual shots to use.

Editing for Composite Images

I first needed to choose the image of Alexa, because she is the main subject. I shot her with three different handbag options, one of which was my favorite to start with, and two backups just in case my initial favorite didn't work out. I like to see other options even when I'm pretty sure which one will be the winner. It just makes me that much more certain that I chose the right shot. When I ended up getting to the final selection stage, it was clear that my favorite was going to work, so I was able to eliminate two thirds of the shots right off the bat. After further selection, I was left with the following three options.

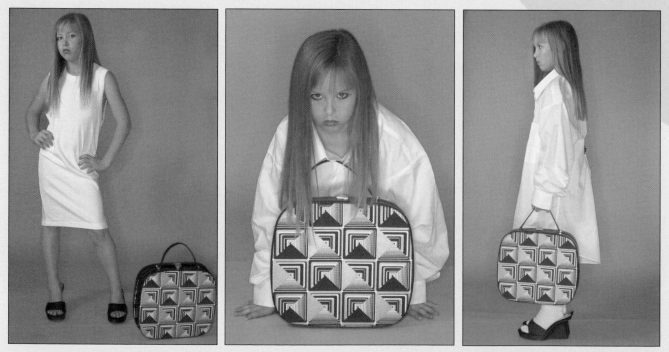

2 Alexa image, option one.   3 Alexa image, option two.   4 Alexa image, option three.

As you can see, I have three very different options for poses.

Option one is of Alexa standing with the handbag separate from her. There are two reasons why I didn't choose this. The first is that she is separated from the bag, and this separation makes the image too complicated, I want Alexa and the bag to be one element. The other reason is that I think she has a little too much attitude, making her seem like she's much older. I needed a face with more innocence.

Option two has a little better expression, and Alexa and the bag are together, but it's still not perfect. Because of her position over the purse, she would appear quite small in the room, and the image would be bottom-heavy.

Option three, which is the one I ended up using, has all the elements I was looking for. The handbag and Alexa are one element, and the expression is much more innocent and soft. I also thought that the "standing at attention" pose in this shot fit in well with the *military* key word I had chosen as part of the concept of the image.

With the subject chosen, it was time to think about the background. The wallpaper used in this image is from the 1970s. It used to be in my bathroom when I was a teenager. My mom, believe it or not, had some left and brought it up to me when I told her I was looking for "retro" wallpaper. I was so excited when I saw what she had pulled for me; it was exactly the strong graphic I was looking for. (This just goes to show that you should never complain about all the "junk" in your parent's attic; you may find it valuable someday!)

Let me back up a moment and give you a little history on this shot. I originally planned to build a full-size set and actually wallpaper the wall. (What was I thinking?) Fortunately, due to time constraints I was unable to accomplish this plan and instead decided to build a miniature wall and floor set, 2.5×2.5 feet, and then place the wallpaper and the model in digitally. (After all, that's what I do, right?) In this case, the time constraint saved me from blindly succumbing to my own creative frenzy and ended up making things a whole lot easier!

The shots of the wallpaper and room were completely straightforward, so it was basically just a question of picking the best exposure. All three shots were photographed under the same lighting conditions, and I had to make sure my main light hit the wall and the model in approximately the same place, even though the wall was very small.

So, after the selection step, I have my three shots: Alexa, the wallpaper, and the room.

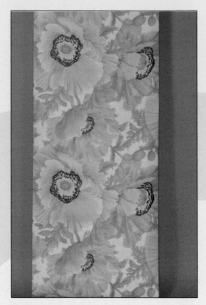

5   The three elements used for the Alexa image.

Compositing

Now that the basic elements are ready, what's the first step in compositing?

It's difficult to work until you have an environment to place the model into, so I usually start compositing by building the rough background out. In this case, I needed to apply the wallpaper to my room. The key point here was to get the wallpaper to look like it's really on the wall—not just superimposed. I used the Blending Modes command to help achieve this effect. This command allows some of the underlying wall's texture to come through in the highlights, giving that touch of realism that makes the room believable. I didn't want viewers to immediately think "digital" when they looked at the room. My goal was to make the room as realistic as possible so that no one would really notice that any digital work had been done.

When the background is in place, the foreground elements can be layered on top. In this case, all I basically needed to do was pop Alexa out of her background and lay her into the image. I finished up with some final work on the shadows and colors.

This image, although simple, shows many of the basic steps of the image creation process: start with a clear story, concept, or message; establish some key guide words to focus your work; select the right image after the shoot; and composite, starting with the background. The following section presents another example of this process, this time with a slightly more complicated image.

Sacred Cow

The next image, "Sacred Cow," is much more complicated. This shot has a lot of elements and had to be produced over the course of several days. Here is the background story for the image.

Preparation

It's the year 4010. There is a planet with a single sacred cow on it. Alien females from a sister planet are in charge of the cow's care and visit to collect her magic milk, which is a cure-all on their home planet.

Okay, I know I'm crazy, but that was the story behind this image. Creating a background story can help you make a composition more coherent, and establishes a framework that can help inspire you and guide your creativity. It also helps you during the editing process, because you are then able to choose elements based on the criteria of how well they help tell your story.

6 "Sacred Cow"

As I mentioned before, during the preproduction phase I like to create a list of words that represent key concepts or messages that the image should convey. Here is my working list for the Sacred Cow:

✿ Hot
✿ Alien
✿ Magic
✿ Future
✿ Tend
✿ Vast

The words on the list are kept in mind during the steps that follow—shooting, editing, and compositing—and help to guide the creative process.

Shooting

The shooting process for this image was spread over several days. We went out to a location in the high desert to get the landscape (and also shot the cow in natural light at the same time). The story of the invisible cow is kind of funny. I had dreamed up this shot years before I actually decided to produce it. Partly because I assumed that the cow would cost me big bucks, I thought I would have to have the cow built by a prop maker. I decided to put in the term *invisible cow* in a search engine and, much to my surprise, the Visible Cow came up. It's a model about 7 inches high and 10 inches long for kids to build. They can see the cow's internal organs and skeleton. It's very educational in its normal state. When I was a kid, I built the "visible women," so I knew basically what I'd be getting. I ordered it and was thrilled. I painted it exactly the way I had seen it in my head and I just absolutely love my cow! Even though she is a small model, she's basically transparent and so only picks up highlights—diminishing my concern to make the lighting match the life-size person. A few days later, we scheduled a day-long shoot with the model, who was shot outdoors against a gray backdrop. We made sure to shoot the model at the same time of day and with the same lighting angle as we had shot the landscape. (Luckily we're in Southern California, where the weather and lighting conditions are pretty much identical 362 days a year.) The UFO was shot outdoors the following day, again under lighting conditions that were as close as possible to the other two shots.

7   Henry, Merit, and the alien cow...all actual size.

Editing for Composite Images

When it came time to go through and pick the shots, I realized I was faced with an embarrassment of riches. The model, Elena, was excellent, so practically every shot was a potential keeper. Unlike the Alexa shot, which had a single main element, however, this image involved several important elements, which all had to fit together correctly when placed in the same image. The edit was not going to be made based on which image looked best in isolation, but instead was going to be made based on which images fit the best when assembled together.

To work out which shots I finally would use, I spent several afternoons playing with different possible layouts, trying different combinations of images in different positions to see which ones looked best. I knew the elements were all excellent, so I just needed to pick the right ones and fit them together. Complicated images are very much like puzzles, finding the correct spot for each piece is very time consuming, but your final image will benefit from this tedious process.

Here are the three mock-ups that I created as part of the editing process. I just do rough cutouts and throw these together without worrying about making perfect masks or anything. I have most of the pieces laid in, except for the tiny little scene under the saucer with our second alien and buckets, which is more of an accessory to the image than a main element.

It is critical at this point to be very aware of the illusion of perspective you are trying to create, and the angle at which each element is shot. The overall perspective of the image is established by the landscape and horizon, which in this case shows that you are seeing a low viewpoint across a flat plain. Because the saucer is a very large object sitting in the medium distance on the plain, you are going to see that object from slightly below, almost edge-on. The closer the saucer is, the lower your view angle is; if the saucer is really far away, you see it almost exactly from the side. Unless the saucer is in a ditch, or you are on a hill, there's no way you should ever be seeing the saucer from above. Photoshop can work miracles, and enables you to cheat perspective a bit by stretching or flattening an object, but it doesn't have the capability to transform an image shot from above into an image shot from below; the right pixels just aren't there. So, as part of the editing process, you have to pick the shots that make each element fit in correctly with the image's virtual perspective grid.

Based on this, I chose my cow and saucer shots based on their angle and had three possible choices for the model. Then I had to decide which milkmaid told the story better. Here's a little insight into the thought process that went into picking the final shot. At this point, I'd been working with the various elements for quite a few hours. After switching back and forth several times between the different options, I decided to get a second opinion. I brought in some people I respect and asked which they thought served the image better. I don't always do this, but in complicated imagery it sometimes helps to have someone with "fresh" eyes take a look. If you've been staring at the same elements for hours and hours, your perspective can get blurred, and you can miss some really obvious things…kind of like how if you repeat the same word over and over again, it eventually starts to sound meaningless.

Option one got a lot of votes because the action involved immediately made a visual connection between the milkmaid and the milk. I agreed, but felt that she wasn't connecting with the rest of the image very well.

No one was really drawn to option two. The standing milkmaid took away from the vast feeling of the landscape. She stood out so much that your eye would stop scanning the rest of the image—kind of like an exclamation point ! smack dab in the middle of the scene. I wanted the image to be more

8   Mock-up option one.

9   Mock-up option two.
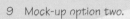

10   Mock-up option three.

homogenous, so that the viewer would scan all the elements in the image instead of focusing on a single thing. Also, the model's expression in Option Two is one of fatigue; she looks like she's working too hard. Instead of tending, she's laboring, which is not what I wanted to convey.

Finally, I decided that option three was the one that really worked for me. I had originally placed her on the left side, in front of the cow, and was not very happy with the resulting lack of visual cohesion between the milkmaid and cow elements. When I moved her behind the cow, it was like magic. You got her connection to the cow: She was with the cow, she wasn't just standing there as an element, and she was participating in the story.

Option one ended up taking a supporting role as the girl loading up the milk onto the saucer. She's a very tiny element, but helps to fill out the story.

Here are the final elements selected for the compositing step (next page).

Compositing

Now that the main elements have been selected, what's next? The first thing I do is spend quite a bit of time painstakingly removing these elements from their background. My masks for each piece are as perfect as possible so that it's just a matter of cleaning up when I place them together. After all the elements have been prepared for compositing, I begin with the background. You should start with the background, because it creates the environment that your various puzzle pieces will be placed into. In this image it's especially important because it sets up how I treat the other pieces that follow. The background determines what colors are reflected onto the objects. The highlights and shadows in each element must reflect the tones that surround it. For instance, the spaceship is very gray with no underlying tone; if the sky is going to be red, however, I must create a red cast on it. It's things such as these that you want to deal with systematically, and you can't do this until your background is done.

11   The first element: A high-desert landscape.

14   The fourth element:
     The exceptionally rare transparent cow.

12   The second element:
     An alien milkmaid.

15   The fifth element: The milkmaid mothership.

16   The sixth element:
     A transparent milk pail.

13   The third element:
     A second alien milkmaid.

The Background

Creating the background required some trial and error. I went through a few variations on the sky before I settled on what felt right. So you can get an idea of the evolutionary process, here are a few of the versions I went through before arriving at the final choice.

Here is where I started. It's a simple combination of sky and ground, just pasting up the two images together. I needed something more dramatic.

I experimented with the Curves adjustment layers, making it darker, but it still wasn't right.

I tried flipping the color and adding more clouds.

I tried making it brighter and more saturated, but it still wasn't alien enough. Also, I decided I liked the original, simpler clouds better. This was just too heavy and busy. Finally, I went back to the trusty set of words I discussed earlier in this chapter. One of my words for this image was *hot*. The environment didn't have to be blazing hot, but it definitely needed to feel very dry and warm—not earthly warm but alien warm. I decided to try a different sky color altogether.

17   Initial landscape with sky.

18   After darkening the landscape and sky.

19   After inverting the colors and adding more clouds using Alien Skin's Xenofex 2 "little fluffy clouds" filter.

20   After saturating and brightening.

21 Back to the original clouds. Add redness.

This was closer, and I knew I was on the right track. It was too pastel and pretty, so I tweaked the sky to be more saturated and less blue. Here is the final outcome.

22 Increased saturation of sky.

Keeping the story and the key words in mind throughout this process helped lead me to a better final outcome. I could have stopped at any point along the way, but the words really helped me to stay focused and follow through until things were really right.

Adding the UFO

Let's move on to the UFO. At this point, I have pasted the elements in and gotten them in the right proportions; however, things are still not quite right. The UFO would have a reddish cast, so using a Selective Color adjustment layer I changed the tones on the upper potion of the saucer.

23 UFO before adding ambient light color.

Now it feels like it's in the scene. This attention to undertones and reflections is key to imaging complicated scenes.

24 UFO after adding ambient light color.

Inserting the Cow

Next, I placed the cow into the shot.

25   Original paste-in of the cow, before fixing color and opacity.

Here is the cow flipped and pasted straight into the scene. She has definitely got a bluish cast, which I'll need to take care of with an adjustment layer. Also, I have used the Blending Modes command and made her Opacity 90% so that she will appear transparent. The problem with this is that she is completely see-through. To fix this, I made another copy of the cow layer and erased everything I wanted to be transparent, leaving just the skeleton at 100% Opacity. The problem with using a blending mode in this particular case was that it was not accurate enough. There are specific parts that had to be solid to make this element look right.

26   After fixing the cow's opacity and adding ambient color.

Studying How Your Elements Relate to Each Other

Of course, we have to look at the size and positioning of the various elements. The visual relationship of the cow to the saucer and the cow to the milkmaid is critical to the overall composition of the image. A lot of trial and error comes into play, and having another opinion can again prove very helpful. Also, you must consider some basic compositional rules. I'm not going to go into detail on the theory of visual composition, but here are a few things to consider when placing the elements:

- **Relative importance.** Are certain elements in the center, in the foreground, or placed in a way to stand out from the rest?

- **Groupings.** What visual cues are given to the connection or relationship between objects by the way they are grouped together?

- **Lines and shapes.** The eye naturally follows and finds pleasing certain geometric patterns, such as linear groupings, circles, and isosceles triangles. Are the elements laid out, relative to each other and the frame of the image, to take advantage of this?

- **Scan pattern.** A viewer's eyes will naturally scan an image from left to right and tend to stop at the right side. Have you taken this into account?

The Milkmaid

With all of this in mind, it's time to add the milkmaid.

At this point, I have pasted in the maid, but the gray backdrop is still showing through her hair, and she needs an even more reddish cast.

I used a Selective Color mask to change the shadows and mid-tones on the hair to match her new background. This is a great way to blend a complicated area such as hair, because it keeps all the little fly-aways and fuzzies, which can be almost impossible to mask correctly.

At this point, I also thought the image still needed a bit more visual detail, so I added a little green implant to the milkmaid's head to establish a visual connection, using color, between her and the milk. I also added in the shadows for all the elements up to this point.

27 Milkmaid pasted in.

28 Maid after using Selective Color to correct the hair.

And Finally, the Milk Pail

As a last step, I created the glowing milk pail.

I followed the same initial steps with the pail as with the cow, adjusting the color cast and fixing the transparency. Also, I used Selective Color to change the cow's milk to green.

29 Before adjusting the milk's color.

30 After using Selective Color
   to change the milk to green.

Finally, I added the glow using the Corona filter from Alien Skin.

The final touch was to add the color around the pail where the green light illuminates the cow and the ground.

Voilá, the alien cow's home world has been created. A composition like this can be a long process, but if you do things in a systematic order your work will go much more smoothly. Again, even though this image was far more complex than the Alexa shot, the basic process was the same: start with a clear story, concept, or message; extract some key words to focus your work; select the right image after the shoot; and composite, starting with the background.

Where We Are

You've prepared, shot, edited, and imaged. Your newest creation is finally complete, and your client is chomping at the bit. Next you'll learn a few important points about how to deliver your latest offspring.

31 After adding the green glow.

32 After adding green reflections from the glow.

Chapter 4

Delivering Your Work

Enthusiastic, excited patrons are banging their spoons on the nice china saying, "Is it soup yet?" Let's serve it up pipin' hot! Present your fancy image casserole to even the most discerning gourmand. Learn how to say "bon appetite" with your own individual style.

Delivery of Images

After all of your shooting and imaging work is done, your deadline is probably fast approaching and you'll need to send off your newest baby to the client.

Because this is the critical part, where you actually get paid, it's important to be clear on this from the start. When I take on an assignment, one of the first questions I ask is, "How do you want this delivered?" Possible answers you may get include CD/DVD, upload to FTP site, email, download from your web site, or delivery of transparencies. All of these methods are acceptable these days; it's just a matter of what your client prefers. (I'll discuss these different delivery methods shortly.)

Another important question to ask is whether the client wants the image flattened or whether they want the main pieces kept in layers. On occasion, I am asked to provide a PSD file with layers. When a model is put onto a background, for example, during the design of the ad the person doing the lay-up type might want some leeway for adjusting the model over to the left or right. In such a case, it's nice for the client to have layers to work with. It can also save your client money because they won't have to come back to you and ask for minor adjustments. This makes them happy, and happy clients come back. Most of the time, however, the client wants the final finished image and doesn't want to deal with layers or flattening; so, normally, I provide flat TIFF and PSD files.

RGB/CMYK

I deliver all of my files in RGB. The reason for this is that the person doing the lay up will usually have direct experience with his or her specific print setup and will be able to do the exact CMYK setup that is required. Because ink setups vary widely, it's impossible for me to do one conversion that's perfect for everything. So, for my clients, I deliver an RGB file along with the proof, which provides a visual reference for what the image should look like when printed. I always explain this to my clients up-front so that they can figure in the time to do the conversions into their schedule. Again, you want these things in writing, so you should have the client sign off that they are responsible for this step in the process and that any color-matching issues that may arise from the conversion to CMYK are their responsibility. The CMYK conversion can significantly affect on the final image. Therefore, make sure the client understands how to handle this. Doing so can prevent a lot of headaches for the photographer or digital artist.

Digital Delivery

A very common way to deliver files is on a CD or DVD. This media avoids the uncertainties of dealing with transferring files over the Internet and gives the client something tangible to hold in their hands. Anything that you send should look appealing and be labeled with the client's name, the job name, the filename, and your copyright info. Don't just write on the disc. Take an extra five minutes to print out a label. It might be a good idea to design your own label branded with your own logo—something you can very quickly change the client and title info on and print when you need it. Everything you send out should represent you at your best. After all, this is what they paid you all that money for…right?

The other way I deliver files is electronically, via the Internet. Some clients want their files FTP'd directly to their server, and this is a great way to work if you're on a tight deadline. You don't have to figure in shipping time, and this delivery method can give your client an extra day to look at the image and make any changes that may be needed. Make sure, when you start the job, that you get all the information you need to FTP to the client. Because there are often small glitches to overcome when attempting FTP delivery, it's very important to upload a small test file to make sure everything will go smoothly when the big delivery day arrives.

Yet another way to deliver files is via email. Sometimes clients who don't have an FTP site set up will ask you to email the files as an attachment. It's always good to create a slightly compressed version with ZIP or SIT, because emailing very large files can be problematic. Make sure you are able to send large files via your email account if this is the form of delivery you agree upon. Some Internet providers have a limit on your mailbox and may not allow you to send large attachments.

> A web site is also great to use as a repository for intermediate images that you need the client to approve as you're working.

Another option is to upload the file to your own web site for the client to come and download. If you create a page with a link to the ZIP or SIT files, the client can come to this page at their convenience and download the file from the job.

As for resolution, I usually am required to supply my clients with a 300dpi file. Occasionally I have been asked to make *much* larger files. One example was a make-up client that wanted to make an 8×10-foot transparency for their show booth. This required an enormous file, that when flattened was about 850MB. Resolution in this case was the key to quality. The reason I mention this is because you will not be able to deliver such an image except on DVD. It's pretty much the only reasonable option. In contrast, I have done some product photography for a make-up line that was strictly for the web. These files were very small, usually JPGs at 72dpi. This entire job was delivered by email quickly and easily. These are the kind of things you need to think about at this stage of the game so that you don't get yourself in trouble later.

Transparencies

Despite the fact that we're now living in a digital age, there have been times over the years that a client has asked me for a transparency. This requires taking the digital image and putting it onto film (which can be done at a service bureau). When they get the transparency, the client is most likely just going to scan the film back to a digital image. Does that make sense? To some photographers it does, because by delivering film they can basically say, "What you see is what you get," and avoid getting involved with any problems the client may have with color matching.

To me, however, it makes no sense to convert a digital image into a transparency just so a client can scan it and make it digital again! It causes loss of quality and, in my opinion, is really just a waste of time and money (especially with recent improvements in color calibration). I suggest you try to talk your client out of this type of delivery if they request it. I have had to talk a couple of clients out of this, and, when convinced that going 100 percent digital was going to work for them, they were quite happy not to incur the extra costs of dealing with transparencies. I haven't had this request in the past year or two now, so it seems that everyone is beginning to embrace digital now as the way to go.

Proofs

Along with any CD/DVD that I ship, I always include a hard copy of what the final output should look like. Image 1 shows an example of a proof.

glitterguru.com Job: HP Proofs ©2003 TROCHE PROOF.

1 Sample of a proof sent to my client Hewlett Packard.

It's important that your proofs look professional. Make sure the job name and your copyright info is included. The filename should also be on the proof, if you are delivering more than one file. This makes figuring everything out much easier for the next person working with the disc. These are actual proofs I use for my clients.

lipgloss_3

eyeshadow_4

lippencils_16c

Base1_54-4

mascara_54_14c

glitterguru.com Job: Milani Cosmetics ©2003 TROCHÉ PROOF

2 Sample of a proof showing multiple files and accompanying filenames.

If I'm delivering the final files electronically via FTP, email, or the web, I ship a proof via overnight delivery. The client can begin laying up the project without it, and the proof will arrive in time for the color matching process.

Printing Proofs

All of my proofs right now are being output on an Epson 2000P, which is an excellent printer that produces high-quality output suitable for proofs. Some clients require other types of prints beside inkjet, and may ask you to provide them "Rainbow" or "Iris" prints to use for color matching. If you need this type of output, you can do a quick search of the Yellow Pages or Internet to locate a local service bureau that can make these kinds of prints for you.

Follow-Up

No matter how you deliver your files, always follow-up. Make a quick courtesy call or send an email to make sure that the file arrived and that the client was able to open it without any problems. It's also your chance to make sure that any other outstanding issues are dealt with and to leave a good final impression with your client as the job concludes.

Where We Are

So far in this journey, you've learned how to create a recipe for an image. You first learned how to gather the necessary ingredients to make it, and then you learned what goes into cooking it and serving it with a bit of flare. So what are you going to do with all of these new culinary skills? In the next chapter, I share with you some insights on how I turn pixels into profit.

Chapter 5

The Business of Photography and Digital Imaging

No punching timecards at the local five-and-dime. Must make money, making art. Psst...here's a peek behind that door that's never open. Come check out how the crazy redhead rubs elbows with the fat guys smokin' cigars. Caution!!! Warning!!! Falling buckets of information ahead. Don't duck, just zip open your noggin and let the knowledge pour in.

If you want to actually put food on the table as a photographer or digital artist, your sales and business skills will be at least as important as your artistic talents. Now, I'm not going to pretend that I'm an expert salesperson, or a world-class business mind, but I have learned—through painful experience—many lessons about what works and what doesn't. In this chapter, I share marketing and business tips that have helped me and continue to be of great value in my career. Hopefully these can save you having to go through your own set of painful experiences and help you on your road to being a successful artist and businessperson.

Marketing

First of all, the most important thing is for people to know that you exist. I know it sounds silly, but it's something that many aspiring artists continually overlook out of shyness or the mistaken belief that the world will beat down a path to find them as they hide out in their studio. We all start out as unknowns, but, unless you want to remain that way, it is critically, vitally important to make people aware of who you are.

In the old days, before email and the Internet, photographers trying to break in to the advertising photography business would take out big ads in books that showcased photographers' work, such as the *Blackbook* or the *Workbook*. Although many ad agencies still use these books to peruse for new ideas, ads cost thousands of dollars, which makes it difficult for someone just starting out (read "broke") to get any exposure. Another way to get work is to get an agent, or rep, to sign you and help get your work into the hands of potential clients. Most agents, however, are constantly bombarded by hopeful artists, and they also tend to be narrow-minded: Unless your portfolio happens to have the specific look that they think is marketable, they often aren't interested.

Technology, however, has made the playing field more even. Email and the web have made it possible to let the world know you're there with little out-of-pocket expense, in the privacy of your bathrobe and slippers. Yes! I am wearing glittery bunny slippers right now.

Email

When I first began working in the field, I would spend 1 to 2 hours every morning doing "email marketing." I used search engines to find art directors, magazines, advertising agencies, and agents. An example search might be "Los Angeles Art Director." Internet directories such as dmoz.org (the Open Directory Project) also have categories for advertising agencies, and I combed these looking for potential clients.

I also kept my eyes open, noticing TV ads, magazine ads, and billboards. If I saw an ad campaign that looked stylistically similar to work I had done, I would search for the agency and art director that produced the campaign and contact them. If no agency was involved, I would go directly to the client showing them a sample of my work in an email and letting them know that I was available for future campaigns.

Most of the time, you can track down a specific email address for the art director or marketing person you want to contact. Failing that, you can at least get the person's name and a general corporate email address. I would write a personal letter to each of these people and include an image from my portfolio in the email. Image 1 is an example of an email that I might send.

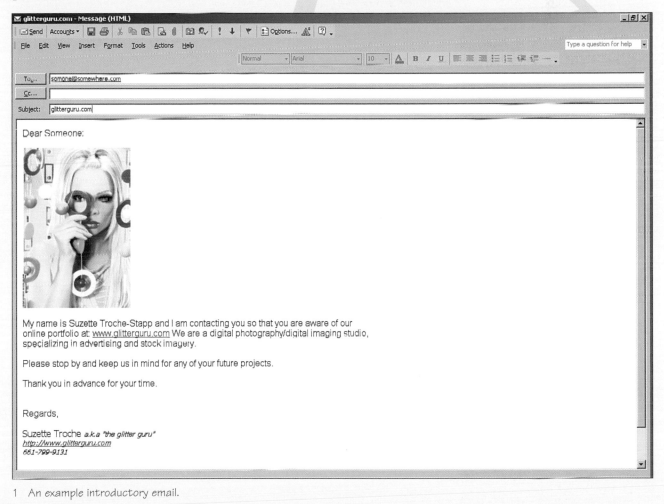

1   An example introductory email.

I send these letters directly to the person whom I think would be interested in using my work, making certain that the letter is customized for the specific recipient. If the email is going to a publication, for instance, I might adjust the letter to include something about a recent story they have published. If you are fortunate enough to have a personal referral to the recipient, "so and so told me to write," make sure to include that as well. It's *very* important that your letters are targeted and personal. I can't stress this enough. If you send bulk emails out without any personal attention, you will be a "spammer" and you will probably upset more potential clients than you will attract. I have sent thousands of these letters over the years and, because they are written to a specific individual, I have received only positive responses.

The example image shows the exact email I would use for soliciting potential clients. I found that a short, casual email, with an eye-catching image embedded within it, got the best response. The image should be small, no larger than 15 to 20KB, and embedded directly in the email, not sent as an attachment.

I can't impress on you enough how powerful email can be. If directed properly, you can make very important people aware of your work and have them keep you in mind for projects they may be assigning or stock they may be purchasing. Jeanne Fulton from Grey Advertising says, "As an art producer (we are now called art producers because we produce photo shoots), I am constantly on the lookout for new and interesting photography, both in the conventional promos and email promos that I receive." This is now an acceptable way to promote your work. One of my big assignment jobs back in 1998 came directly from a letter such as this; they called and said, "I have an assignment that's just right for you!" I never even sent the art director my portfolio; they just assigned the job based on the images they saw online. Pretty amazing!

The other key component to this type of marketing is targeting the right people. This means some work on your part. Look at their work and see whether it fits in with your style. Smaller agencies, especially, often have a specific style they tend to use in their work, so it's important to see that they use your kind of imagery. Don't send someone who does a lot of work in color still lifes of food your link to a bunch of black-and-white pictures of bald women! Make sure you feel confident that this person will respond to what you have to offer. Taking the time to make a good match is what makes this tool really powerful. The great part about this search is it can take you all over the country and the world without ever leaving home or spending one dime on postage!

Also, if you are looking for representation, introductions via email can be a good way to solicit agents.

The Web

The other component to this type of marketing is your online portfolio. Having an easy-to-navigate, good-looking, clean, no-fuss web site is incredibly valuable. First, try to pick a domain name that's easy to remember, either because it's descriptive (such as your name) or because it's catchy. Avoid dashes, unusual spellings, and .net domains.

Something to take into consideration when constructing your site is maintenance. It's very important to have a site that you can make changes to yourself or at a fairly low cost, because having a web site that's current is part of what makes it a useful tool. That's why, in my opinion, simple no-fuss web sites can be a better tool than the fancy ones with Macromedia Flash and music. If you can build a fancy site yourself, that's fine; if you can't and you wind up needing to shell out hundreds of dollars to change a couple of images, however, you'll be sorry later. A simple site is also generally quicker to download, which is something your visitors will appreciate. Even though you can assume that most people you care about at ad agencies or corporations will have high-speed connections, leave out the fluff and use the bandwidth for putting up high-quality jpegs (100 to 150KB) of your portfolio.

Keep your site fresh. If someone you've contacted does happen to bookmark your site, which is what you are hoping for, it is nice when that person comes back to have some new images for him or her to look at. I try not to remove too much when I update. I usually add three or four new images and just remove maybe one or two. That way if they are coming back to see something again, it will most likely still be up online. I try to update the site at least every month if not more often. Use your updates as an opportunity to email the people who have responded to your initial letter with interest. This keeps you fresh in their minds, which is half the battle when that job comes across their desk. Also, avoid having any "under construction" areas in your site; just omit the section until the content is ready. Image 2 shows the sample portfolio page from my site. All the image icons are down the left, and the images appear in the frame on the right when clicked.

2 An example web site, www.glitterguru.com.

Web Site Sections

As you can see, I have several different sections on my site. Standard sections you will probably want to include are Portfolio, Before and After, Biography, News, Advice, Contact, and Stock.

Here's a rundown for each of the sections.

Portfolio

This is pretty self-explanatory. This is where I have all my images for prospective clients to come and view my work. It should be easy to navigate and load quickly. Also, on each image page you should provide the proper credits. Image 3 shows an example.

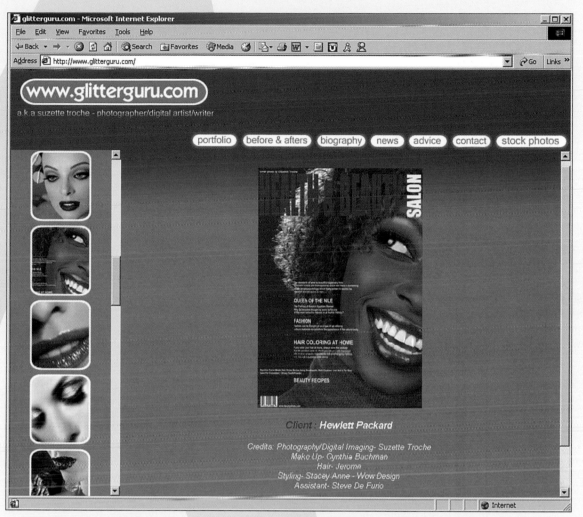

3   Example Portfolio page.

I believe strongly that all those who worked on a photo shoot should have their names prominently displayed with a link to their web sites. This has several advantages: You keep your team happy by giving them credit where it's due, you show prospective clients specifically which parts of the project you had a hand in, and you show that you can work with a team. Also, you should include a copyright notice on every web page that has one of your images:

> All images on this website are ©2003 Troche-Stapp and may not be reproduced without permission.

For more information on creating high-impact digital portfolios, I recommend *Designing a Digital Portfolio*, by Cyndi Baron, which should be hitting the shelves in December 2003.

Before and After

This section is *crucial* to anyone who is showing digitally created images. Clients are thrilled to see this kind of demonstration of your abilities. Images 4 and 5 show examples of a Before and After page. Image 6 shows an example of image compositing.

Basically these pages show how the images were transformed or constructed. The work involved can range from retouching to total image compositing.

4   An example Before and After Page

5   An example Before and After page.

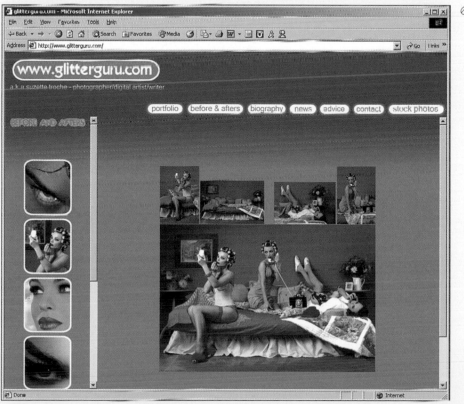
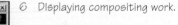

6   Displaying compositing work.

Another example of an excellent Before and After section is on the site of the very talented Thomas Herbrich (http://www.herbrich.com/), shown in Image 7 and Image 8.

7   A Portfolio page from Thomas Hebrich's web site.

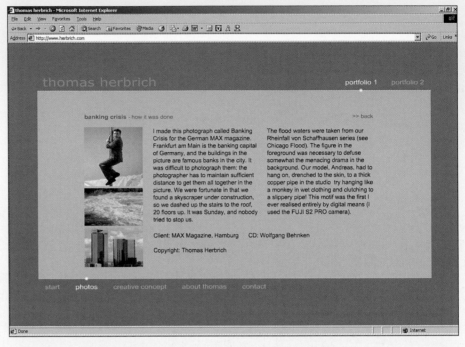

8   A Portfolio page from Thomas Hebrich's web site.

Thomas believes, as I do, that "secrets are unprofessional." His web site clearly demonstrates how his images are constructed, which shows prospective clients how his studio works. I urge you to take a look at his site for inspiration.

Biography

This is pretty self-explanatory. It's about you! Make it conversational, not a resumé of uninteresting facts. This a good place to let your personality come through. It's also a good idea to include a picture of yourself so that people can attach a face to the name. Include your email address so that people can email you from this page. They just read about you; now they might want to contact you. Make it easy for them to do it.

News

This is a good place to keep people up-to-date on what you're working on or shooting.

Here are some examples from my news page:

- **6-27-2003.** Look in this week's *Entertainment Weekly* magazine for Suzette's pictures of Kathy Griffin on the "It List."
- **11-07-2002.** Suzette has just wrapped shooting a series of images for comedienne Kathy Griffin. These images will be used for a spot on *The Late Late Show* with Craig Kilborn, airing November 14.
- **9-20-2002.** Check out this month's issue of *Picture Magazine*. Suzette is interviewed by Scott Kelby and Adobe. On newsstands now.

This kind of info lets the industry know that you're working! You aren't sitting around waiting for them to call. Anything can be news if it's phrased right!

Advice

This section correlates with my column "Advice from the Glitterguru: Sage Advice for the Photoshop Fiend" that runs in *PEI* magazine. Remember, your web site is there to advertise your talents and latest endeavors, so use it!

Plus, people just love free content, so if you have something to offer besides examples of your work, chances are, people will visit more frequently.

Contact

This is a very important section that should be as thorough and as complete as possible. On my web site, for instance, I have the following information:

- Complete contact information for myself, including phone and fax numbers and email addresses
- Contact information for all the people I work with, including makeup artists, hairdressers, stylists, and prop people
- Contact information for my representation, including information on my literary agent and my publisher

Stock

If you are going to sell stock imagery like I do, you'll want a place to show it. The web is ideal for this purpose. When you click the Stock button from the navigation bar, a page comes up asking you to either log in or fill out a form to request a password. The reason for this is I like to know who is looking at my stock images. Also, when they're in that area, those persons browsing the images have the option to save the images they may be interested in to a "light box" for future reference. This is very convenient for the person viewing all these images and provides me with valuable information for the future. I keep a database of all the visitor's information. Because I know what kind of images they are interested in, I can email them in the future when I have new images for them to view.

Portfolios

Even in this digital age, many art directors will want to see your actual portfolio before they hire you. Internet marketing and email may get them interested, but it's your portfolio (and your ability to "sell" yourself personally) that will close the deal.

Your portfolio will constantly be a work in progress. Even so, there will always be a few shots that are liked by just about everyone and will become standbys. Surprisingly, you may find that the images you're not particularly crazy about are sometimes the most commercially successful. That's why it's important to be as objective as possible when choosing images for your portfolio. Don't fill it up with images that you are emotionally attached to but that no one would ever buy. As commercial artists, we need to appeal to a diverse group of people, so it's important that your work have a definitive style but at the same time a range that makes you marketable. After all, the idea is to be able to pay the rent *and* create art, so this is the point where the business side should take over.

The hardest part about creating a portfolio is that to be really successful, it must strike a delicate balance between several opposing forces: You want it to have a definite style but also show your creative range; you want the images to be commercially marketable, but you want to be original and avoid looking like everyone else.

For some great advice, consider what some of the leaders in the field have to say. First, here's what Bill Harper, art director extraordinaire, has to say about his attitude toward portfolios:

> "Finding the right photographer (especially one in the digital manipulation arena) is a bit of a crapshoot. The real issue: Okay, so they have some neat stuff in their book. Question is, will they be able to translate what I have in my head onto the page? Moreover, will they be able to help make it even better? Can they surprise me? In the right way? (Because nothing is worse than being surprised in the wrong way.)

> "The second issue is: How much of this is actually theirs? Why? Because handholding is a pain in the ass. As for books, the review process begins by trying to find cool ideas that show some originality of thought and style.

> "There are a lot of "me too" digital photographers (or regular ones for that matter). If you look long enough, you can find the ones who show real creativity in their samples."

Next, let's hear from Klaus Luca. Klaus is a photographer of great renown, and has captured images of celebrities such as Jack Nicholson, Marlene Dietrich, Mohammed Ali, Sting, and Lauren Bacall (to name a few). He also has long-established working relationships with magazines such as *Interview, Town & Country, GQ, Harper's Bazaar*, and *Vogue*. Klaus was kind enough to share his insights on portfolios:

> "It's impossible to have finished ads in a new artist's book. Don't use dummy ads because agency art directors do them so much better and you might give a bad first impression, so stay with photographs. This is a very competitive business, so specialize in what you like most; otherwise you might spread yourself too thin. Creating a portfolio is the first and most important step in promoting yourself in this field.

> #1 Never put a bad image into the portfolio; less is more, and one bad image can lower the quality of all your images, because that is what your clients remember.

> #2 Don't judge any of your photographs for the amount of effort and time put into it; the one with the least effort might be the best in your book.

#3 Don't divide the book by photos and ads or black-and-white and color, but separate by subject matter.

#4 If you feel you don't have enough images, don't take photos of one shoot and disburse them over the book; you can't fake it. It leaves a bad impression, even if the images are great. Leave them together to make it a series or study of one subject.

"Most important: Start off with a bang and leave off with a bang—meaning your client will remember the first few images and the very last images the most. So don't start off weak and build up. Put your best forward immediately; give them something memorable to think about. Less is more, content and quality counts; there is no substitute for it."

Fellow Photoshop guru Chris Tarantino gives this advice:

"Having a great portfolio is half the battle in pursuing work. It could even possibly be the clincher for getting work over a competitor; however, word of mouth gets you into a lot of doors that you may not have even heard of. It can also close those same doors. It always pays to be caring and conscientious about your work. I have a pretty healthy list of clients that I have done work for, but no one knows about them until the portfolio is sent out. The most satisfying times in my career are when I've come home and there are job offers on my answering machine from people whom I have never heard of.

"I have two portfolios, one online and one bound nicely in a leather portfolio. The one that gets the most use by far is the online version. Even so, you must have both. Once you start marketing yourself, you'll get requests to send your book out, to agencies and clients, so be ready. Remember, how your pictures are presented can give them more or less value. If someone has something in their hands that looks and feels rich or expensive, they are more likely to take it seriously. There's also something to be said for being unique; so pick your portfolio wisely, because it says a lot about who you are before someone even opens the cover."

Klaus Luca has the following comments on his portfolio presentation:

"I have two mini-books, which are 8 1/2 inches wide by 5 1/2 inches high and spiral bound. I also have the large book, which is 13 inches high by 19 inches wide. This is a bound book made to specification by the House of Portfolios. It has a matte see-through acrylic cover, so you can get an impression of the first image peeking through. The first page is a compilation of the small images of the whole book and has a different order than the two mini-books. My most successful portfolio was a mini-harmonica foldout about 3 inches wide and 4 inches high; it included about 100 images, and totally wowed and overwhelmed the client."

Also, it's important to have some kind of promo material to put in the back pocket of the portfolio. *Promo cards*, as they are called in the industry, are printed materials that you include in the back pocket of your portfolio for the customer to keep. They can come in any shape or size, from a single 5×8 inch card to a small book, but always basically consist of the same things: your images and your contact information. Create a promo card that accentuates the image of your "brand"—fitting in with your own personal style. You want to see those promo cards gone when the book comes back. This means there may have been some immediate interest, or that they wanted to keep you on file for future projects.

Klaus says:

"With the portfolio, I always include a bio, any awards, and a list of past clients. The leave-behind card that I include has most images that are in the portfolio. Just imagine how many portfolios an art buyer or art director looks at every month; it all becomes blurry. So, the leave-behind becomes a crucial part of your portfolio presentation. I have seen all kinds of leave-behinds, from mini-portfolios to cards to posters and so forth."

You're on- and offline portfolios should be similar but not identical. In other words, don't put exactly the same thing both in the portfolio and on the web site. That way, when people get your book or view the site, they will see something new, different, and, you hope, interesting.

Also, make sure your prints are excellent! Whatever type of printer you use, make sure that the images are on excellent-quality photo paper and that the prints have good highlight and shadow detail. Also, give all your images uniform sizes; this really helps make your book feel more together.

Professional opinions on your portfolio are priceless. One way to get feedback is to talk to people who have requested your book and ask them what they thought about your presentation. Very often the person who viewed your book will gladly give you his or her opinion. Another way to get a professional opinion is through your local chapter of the Advertising Photographers of America (APA, http://apanational.org/). APA offers portfolio reviews: For a small fee (usually around $55), a photographer's rep will meet with you and take a look at your work. If you are just starting out or your portfolio isn't getting you the assignments you want, the opinion of these professionals may shed some light as to why.

Estimating the Job

Okay, now you have your foot in the door and they want you to give them an estimate for a project! OMG! What now? First off, the most important question to ask is, "What's your budget?" This is vital, but a lot of people just don't ask. I would say 90 percent of the time I get an answer, and it's really helpful in putting together a sensible estimate. There are many ways to put together a shoot. If you find out it's a large budget, for example, you can go with top models who make thousands a day; if it's a small budget, however, you can go to smaller agencies where talent is less expensive. A lot of things in a production can rack up costs. Suppose, for instance, they want a shot of a snowy landscape as part of the composite, but you live in California. If there's a large budget, you would figure travel expenses to a place that's currently got snow; if the budget is smaller and does not have enough to cover travel, however, you may have to shoot a model of a snowy scene or perhaps even use a stock image.

Working to make the image happen within the project's budget will make art directors very happy. Their goal is to create the shot they envision with the resources they have. Sometimes this isn't always possible. I've been approached to estimate jobs and when I ask the magic question I found out there was literally no budget. In these cases, the question just kept me from wasting a lot of my time and resources putting together an estimate. There have been other times when I have gotten a comp and a budget and, after doing the math, realized that there would not be enough money to do the shot properly (not to mention provide me with compensation for usage). Why waste your time? There are ways to cut corners, but not at the expense of your reputation. Make sure whatever you decide to do still provides the client with top-quality work, and turn down projects that you think can't be done properly with the budget provided.

Now let's talk about profit. Obviously, you want to make something for all the work you're going to do. As far as estimating the photography, you should determine your rate by the scope of the project, not on an hourly basis. Tell your client that the usage they will license is the biggest factor in how much your fees will be. In other words, if you were shooting a beauty campaign that will run in a local paper, your rate would be dramatically lower than for an image that would appear in a national ad campaign. Usage is how you determine what your photographic fees are.

Licensing

Generally speaking, in "assignment" work the client receives an exclusive license for use of the image you have created for them for a specific length of time. I've had assignments with licenses that span a range of 1 year to 5 years of "exclusive use." What is exclusive use? Exclusive use means that no one else can use the image for the length of time the client purchases it for. Often there will be an option for the client to purchase additional years of licensing at a set rate. The other factor specified under the license is the "usage," which details how and where the image will be used. Some examples of different usage types include print ad campaign, direct mail, online/web, collateral for brochures, and outdoor for billboards. Usage is also classified according to the region covered, such as international, national, and regional. The license fee is negotiated based on the length of the license, the type of usage, and the area of distribution. For instance, a national magazine ad campaign will pay quite a bit more than a trade magazine campaign.

Stock Work

Let's talk about stock for just a moment. Stock can be either something you've shot and imaged on your own, or it can be an assignment project whose license has expired. In contrast to assignment photography, where the client pays the expenses, license fee, and creative fees, with stock you generally pay the expenses out of your own pocket, hoping to license the image later. On rare occasions, an agency will ask you to create an image on "spec." What this usually means is that they will pay the expenses but no fees or licensing until the image is sold. Stock is licensed the same way as assignment. Your fee should be based on where the image will be used and for how long. Stock imagery is now where I make most of my income. It's a great way to work because you have total artistic freedom. I of course have to keep in mind what's marketable and create images that consistently have my style mark imprinted on them. I have several regular clients who come to me for my imagery that I shot with them in mind, but I still have the final word on all of my work.

Model Release

In all of these cases, you must get a model release. There are many kinds of releases, from a limited release to a buy-out. Most of my models sign a buy-out release. Because I shoot mostly stock, I never know what an image might be used for. I must have a release that allows me to use the image anywhere, anytime. A great resource for model releases is the APA.

Copyright

No chapter on business tips would be complete without mentioning copyright. This is important. Generally speaking, the copyright to all the images you create belongs to you, unless specified otherwise in your contract. This is why the license is necessary. It gives the client and agency permission to use the image in a certain way for a certain length of time. Because you own the copyright, after the license expires you have the right to do with the image as you please. At no time does copyright change hands.

You should watch out for a few key phrases: *Work-for-hire*, *buy-out*, or any reference to *transfer of copyright* should be a big red flag. All of these terms are saying there will be some kind of transfer of ownership. As a general rule, you never want to do this. Always license your images, keeping ownership of the copyright for yourself. Clients will often demand a buy-out. Do not let them have it! Keeping ownership of your own work allows you to build a library of images you own, which can potentially earn money for you again and again in the future. Without this ownership, you're just doing "work for hire" and going paycheck to paycheck with no hope of ever building up substantial residual income. Usually, pricing a buy-out on the high end keeps the client from pushing for it. If the client is insistent, push for a longer license period instead. Most clients won't really need an ad for more than a few years anyway. Offer to give them a 5-year license for the price of the 3-year license, they'll love you for it and feel they are getting a deal. Negotiate with the client on license terms if you have to, but don't part with copyright unless your electricity is getting shut off, you're going to be evicted, or the vet is about to repossess your dog.

Ownership of Copyright

Here is a touchy area: ownership of copyright when a photographer and digital artist work together. I'm lucky to do both parts, so it's rarely an issue for me. When I work with other photographers, however, I always deal with the topic of copyright and licensing fees right up front.

Currently, the law is unequal in its treatment of photographers versus digital artists: Photographers have an established legal precedent that says they always own the copyright to their images, digital artists who work on those images do not. This is why it is critical as a digital artist to negotiate copyright ownership with the photographer based on your input to the final image.

Suppose, for instance, that a photographer brings me in to retouch something without doing major changes to the image. In this case, I would not ask for copyright ownership on the image, but would just base my fee on my hourly rate. Here is another scenario: The ad agency has a concept for a final image involving several elements (for instance, a model, a background, and some props). The photographer is hired to shoot the elements, and I am then brought in to create a complete image using the individual elements. On a job like this, I ask for half the copyright and half the license fees on top of my hourly fee.

Most photographers don't like this. But when you look at it objectively, is it really fair for one person to get 100 percent of the ownership when the other person is doing 50 percent (or more) of the work? In the songwriting industry, if two people create a composition, they both own the publishing rights for that song. Shouldn't it be the same when two people compose an image together? Unfortunately, as a digital artist, if you don't stick up for yourself you'll wind up with the short end (or no end) of the stick. It's up to you to protect your rights and negotiate a fair and equitable copyright ownership agreement.

Real-World Job Breakdown for Digital Artists

Here is a sample breakdown of fees from an actual job in which I did the digital imaging and someone else did the photography:

Job description:
> 1 image composed of 6 elements, in 2 billboard sizes. Shot on 21/4 and delivered on CD in RGB format. For use in national advertising campaign and direct mail. (See license.)

Expenses and model's fees:
> $32,500

Photographer's fee:
> Prep day: $5,000
> 3 days of shooting: $21,000

Digital imaging:
> $500 per hour with 20 estimated hours: $10,000

Licensing:
> PERMITTED USES OF IMAGES UNDER THIS LICENSE
> The image or images covered by this License may be used by Licensee for the following purposes only (hereinafter Permitted Uses): National Advertising Campaign and Direct Mail; English language rights only.

License fee:
> 5 years: $20,000
> Additional years for same usage may be purchased at a rate of $4,000 per year.

On this job, I was closely involved from the outset. The photographer and I did the storyboard breakdown and estimate together as well as preproduction (props, sets, costumes, crew, and casting). I also provided consulting during the shoot to ensure that the elements would fit together properly. After the shoot, I put the image together and had responsibility for delivering the job on time and to the art director's satisfaction.

Based on my close involvement with the project, I negotiated a 50 percent split of copyright ownership on the final image. Even with this split, the photographer still ended up with more money, taking home $36,000 as compared to the digital artist's fees of $20,000. If we hadn't split the copyright (and therefore the licensing fees), however, the split would be an even more inequitable—$46,000 to $10,000. The other major benefit, for a digital artist, of splitting the copyright is the possibility of residual licensing fees should the client buy extra years, or should the image be sold as stock when the client's license expires. With a 50 percent split, the two artists split any license fees that come in later and have to both agree on to whom it is licensed and for how much. Without copyright ownership, the digital artist has no chance of recurring fees and no control over the use of the image.

Why this is not commonplace is apparent: The photographers out there do not want the digital artist to own half of their images and take a bigger piece of the pie. However, digital artists are a critical part of the creative team, and many projects rely on their creative abilities to succeed.

I believe someday the equitable splitting of fees and ownership will be the norm. Until then it is up to you to protect your financial and artistic interests. Personally, if I cannot negotiate what I consider to be a fair splitting of the copyright ownership, I would rather turn work away.

On the digital end, I prefer to work by the hour. I give excellent estimates on my time and I am usually within an hour or two of my estimate every time. I prefer to charge for digital this way; it's just easier for changes and additions that may occur later on in the project.

Estimate Versus Bid

There are two different terms used in this industry: estimate and bid. Estimates are flexible, but bids are fixed. Therefore, be very clear on what you're getting into when a client asks for you to quote a price.

With an estimate, you are stating in good faith what you believe the cost will be to do the job. This means you are estimating the fees and the expenses, and you will most likely be asked to provide receipts. If you come in under budget, you bill the client the lower amount. Likewise, if you go over budget (within reason), you can bill the client for what the job actually ended up costing.

If you are asked to bid a job, you give a set fee, and no matter what your actual expenses turn out to be, this is what you charge.

Estimating a job involves taking into account every expense you will incur; so unless you've done it before, it can be quite complicated. Fortunately, there are software packages available with prebuilt templates to help you prepare an estimate. Two packages I recommend are FotoBiz (www.fotobiz.net) and the estimating/invoicing package from the APA.

9   Preparing an estimate with prebuilt templates.

Life is a lot easier with a software program such as these to help you out. It reminds you of all the things that you may need going into a shoot. From insurance to travel, everything has a line item. An estimate summary makes it very easy for the client to see what they are being charged for each item. You also can provide them with a detailed printout, which breaks down everything much further than just the summary pages shown here.

The estimate/invoice serves as your work order and contract, and the second page (not shown here) includes all the legal boilerplate about cancellation and so forth.

For more estimating resources, you can check out *www.fotoQuote.com* and the APA Survey. (Both of these resources require you to either purchase the software or become a member of the organization.) Keep in mind these are just reference materials, however. So although they may be valuable as a starting point to work from, you need to look at the specifics of the job presented to you.

Photographer Jeff Sedlik, who is world famous for his portraits of jazz greats such as B. B. King, Dizzy Gillespie, and Miles Davis, has this final bit of advice:

> "When it comes to the business of image making, many photographers are short-sighted. They focus intently on the creative or logistical challenges of the assignment, but are fuzzy on its financial details. While skimming quickly over the fine print on a purchase order, they fail to realize that the primary goal of negotiating is not to win the immediate assignment. Instead, it is to win the respect of the client with whom a long-term relationship will result in job after job for years to come.

> "To do this, you must find a solution that satisfies the needs of both your business and theirs. Then make darn sure that you create powerful images. Your photographs must not only satisfy the requirements of the project at hand, but also be versatile enough to inspire the client to license the images for additional usage, and to present stock usage opportunities after the initial usage period expires. What's the nine-letter key to success? N-E-G-O-T-I-A-T-E."

Where We Are

Well, that about wraps up the first half of this book, in which the focus was on high-level concerns such as getting work, storyboarding, image breakdowns, and general career organization. You may have noticed that Part I didn't contain a lot of imagery. Part II will be the complete opposite. We'll open Photoshop and delve into the theory behind the making of images—showing examples from actual jobs. Follow me into the land of make believe.

Chapter 6

Beauty Retouching

Lights, camera, action. Time to turn the glitz on and spin raw beauty into pure perfection. Take a peek at Tinsel Town's newest plastic surgeon. Watch this glittery gal perform virtual nose jobs, eye-lifts, and collagen injections right before your very eyes. Put on your shiny, bright lab coat and accompany me on my rounds. Get geared up to gain your Ph.D. in pretty pixels...beware flawless faces ahead!

Disclaimer

I want to preface this section with a disclaimer. *All* the women in this chapter are *perfect* before I touch a pixel. They are smart, charismatic, and incredibly beautiful inside and out. These gorgeous women are human, however, and that is no longer acceptable in today's beauty and fashion world. I am asked to make them superhuman, perfect beyond reality. On the upside, I do *love* to make beautiful women into super-beautiful women, and that's important because retouching is often the meat and potatoes of the jobs I do.

Styles of Retouching

I like to think of retouching techniques as falling into three different styles or categories: reality retouching, plastic surgery, and fantasy. These categories serve an artistic purpose. By establishing a goal for the ultimate look and feel of the image, they provide the parameters that decide the range of techniques I'm willing to use and give me the boundaries for the job at hand.

As I've mentioned in previous chapters, it's very important to have a concept of where you're trying to go before you start working. This is especially true for retouching—you don't want to just go in and start hacking away! Deciding in advance what kind of style you're aiming for will keep your work focused and help you produce a more unified final image.

These categories also prove quite helpful when working with clients. You can show them the range of possibilities, including before and after images to illustrate each style, to give them an idea of what they can expect to see when you're done. This helps ensure the client will understand the process and be satisfied with the end result.

If your portfolio doesn't have examples of all the different styles in it, you can use examples from magazines to get across the different possibilities. I suggest trying to incorporate these different styles into your portfolio, however, because it will help you broaden your client base and give you more work opportunities.

Reality Retouching

Reality retouching is the kind of retouching you do when the client doesn't want anyone to know that you have altered the image. I find this style of retouching the most challenging, because there is an art to having your work go completely unnoticed. When doing this style of retouching, we usually don't remove every wrinkle, but instead just make the subject more attractive. What do I mean by "more attractive"? Well, it's subjective, but I like to concentrate on the idea of removing what's distracting me from the person I'm retouching. In real life we are animated, and this makes those little lines and spots much less noticeable. In fact, the little imperfections, as part of a real-live person, can add character and charm. When you freeze a moment in time and give the eye a chance to concentrate on these minor imperfections, however, they become more pronounced. This is where reality retouching comes in. The idea is to do the minimal amount of work necessary to lessen those slight imperfections. Among the things that you'll want to work on are blemishes that need removing, deep wrinkles that need softening, tired eyes that need whitening, and yellow teeth that need to be brightened.

Reality retouching (see Image 1) is also the first step in retouching for a large majority of my images. It establishes a foundation upon which to do fantasy retouching and plastic surgery.

1 Before and after images showing reality retouching.

RefleXXions
EYES
"A Whole New Kind Of Reflection"

Plastic Surgery

Another category of retouching is plastic surgery. This is where you really transform the person, perhaps even removing years from the person's face, by lifting and altering her features. Plastic surgery can involve drastic changes: nose jobs, eye-lifts, liposuction, and hair extensions. However, the goal is still to achieve the desired result without making the person look completely unrealistic.

2   Before and after images showing a plastic surgery eye-lift.

3   Before and after images showing a plastic surgery nose job.

Fantasy Retouching

The final category I use is fantasy retouching. This is where things start to get a little surreal. With a fantasy retouch, you're no longer trying to imitate reality or conceal your work. In fact, the effect you create will become an integral artistic component of the whole image, and almost anyone looking at the image will immediately realize that it has been artificially enhanced.

Many times, when you retouch this intensely, you almost turn the model into a painted figure. When you do this, you'll probably want to extend this look out to the whole image, creating a dreamy surreal quality so that the retouched model still looks as though she fits into her surroundings. As you'll see later, this kind of effect can be achieved in an image by playing with light, color, or focus.

4   Before and after images showing fantasy retouching.

AVOIDING BEGINNERS' MISTAKES

A few things jump out when I see a bad retouching job. First and foremost is when I see a face on which parts of the skin have been retouched and other parts haven't. Also, remember your edges! The edges of anything are key to making something look "right"; so if you blur the edge of a lip line too much while retouching, it will look wrong. Working evenly and paying attention to your edges will keep you from making beginners' mistakes.

This chapter will give examples of each of the three categories I've defined. As usual, you can find the images used in this chapter on the web site, so you can try things out for yourself.

This discussion starts first with reality retouching, which is not only a useful technique in and of itself, but forms the basis for the more advanced styles.

Reality Retouching

Reality retouching should be invisible. Your mission is to be as stealthy as possible—get in and out without being detected. You will probably not receive any credit for this mission because nobody's supposed to know about it. You, your client, and your team (if any) are the only ones who will receive the quiet satisfaction of a job well done.

For the first example, consider an image that was designed as a point of purchase (POP) display for Reflexxions. As is typical with makeup companies, the client wants the girl in the display to look as natural as possible, while still being "perfect"—definitely a job for reality retouching.

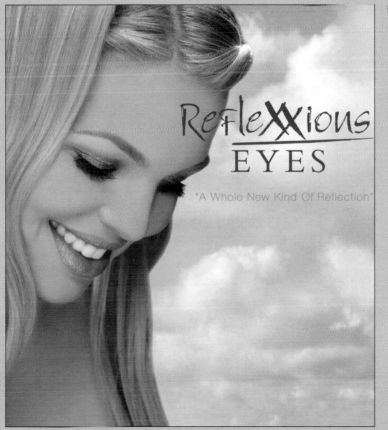

5   An example of reality retouching.

Assessing the Image

It's important to start by assessing the image as a whole, and deciding more or less what you want to do beforehand. Working with the image on the screen, make notes of the areas that need to be changed. By taking the time to do this assessment before "jumping right in," you will develop a clearer mental image of the final product. This will keep you from over- or under-doing any one area and will help you produce a better-balanced final image. It's a good idea to have a mental checklist that you go over when assessing the image. Here's an example check list:

- Overall skin (including forehead, nose, cheeks, chin, and jaw)
    - Smooth the texture, remove bumps or major wrinkles.
    - Even out the color, conceal and blend blemishes or uneven makeup.
    - Remove any unwanted shininess.
- Hair
    - Eliminate any fly-aways.
    - Fill in gaps.
    - Fix color on roots.
- Eyebrows
    - Check overall shape. Reshape if necessary.
    - Corral any loose or wild hairs.
    - Divide unibrow.
- Eyes
    - Brighten whites of eyes.
    - Check for and remove mascara clumps.
    - Check for crow's feet, and blend away as needed.
    - Soften under-eye circles.
    - Remove unwanted or distracting catch lights.
- Nose
    - Even out or blend away unwanted shadows on sides of nose.
- Lips
    - Check shape of lips. Define and reshape as necessary.
    - Clean up bleeding lipstick.
    - Clean up and even out highlights on lips.
- Teeth
    - Whiten teeth.
    - Correct slightly crooked teeth.
- Cheeks, chin, and jaw
    - Lessen deep smile lines or wrinkles.
    - Smooth evenness of blush on apple of cheek.
- Body parts (legs, arms, and so on)
    - Smooth tone and texture.
    - Improve contours of highlights and shadows.

As part of your assessment, decide what to leave and what to remove so that the job is believable. Often art directors will give you specific guidelines for what they'd like to see done. On this particular job, I worked closely with the art director to decide what to remove and fix. Image 6 shows the art director's marks indicating the changes she wanted made. As you can see from all the marks, there's a lot of work to be done for something that's supposed to look natural!

After going over the raw image with the art director, I then begin the basics of retouching.

6 The marked-up image showing changes requested by the art director.

Removing Wrinkles

Before you even think about touching your Tool palette, be sure to duplicate your original layer. To do this, right-click the layer and select Duplicate Layer. Name the layer **model copy**. Work on the copy layer, and leave your original layer untouched. That way you will always have a copy to go back to for reference. I usually begin by using the Healing Brush tool to remove small wrinkles and any stray hairs that may have moved over the face during the shoot.

KEEPIN' IT REAL: 1

Don't eliminate all the wrinkles when cleaning up the skin. If the person is smiling and you take away all the wrinkles, it will look odd and unnatural. Be aware of what you remove and make sure it's not crucial to the expression in the face. You also can quickly assess your work by turning on and off the retouching layer. This is a visual aid in identifying unnatural changes.

7   Removing the forehead wrinkle using a small brush.

KEEPIN' IT REAL: 2

When working with the Healing Brush, if you want to lessen but not remove the wrinkles completely, go to the Edit menu and select Fade Healing Brush. You can use the slider to lessen the effect of the brush and bring back some of the natural wrinkles.

8   The Fade Healing Brush dialog box.

Start by choosing a brush just big enough to cover the area that needs to be eliminated. You can use the left and right bracket keys ([and]) to reduce or increase the brush size.

For the type of wrinkle shown here, which is small and very linear, click one end of the wrinkle, hold down the Shift key (which makes the tool work in a straight line), and click to the end of that wrinkle line. You also can use small short strokes with the tool to accomplish the same effect.

Next, using the same technique, work on any stray hairs covering the face. Continue this process until you have eliminated all of these fine lines, hairs, and wrinkles.

Flawless Skin

I like to retouch in a little different way than most people. I discovered, when I started looking through the different channels to find out where all the garbage was hidden, that generally speaking on Caucasian models the "junk" can be seen more readily in the Green channel. (For other ethnicities, it may be seen more readily through one of the other channels.) To highlight those bad areas that I need to concentrate on, I open a window (Window > Documents > New Window) with a view of the Green channel, in addition to my view of the full-color version. As you can see in the image, this Green channel view helps you to see those areas of rough skin texture more easily. Note that in the Green channel window, even though you're only looking at the Green channel, you want all the channels to be active. Otherwise, when you retouch, you'll be painting in the color green only. Active channels appear highlighted in the Channels palette as seen in Image 10.

To activate all channels while viewing only the Green channel, go to the Channels palette and click the RGB channel. Then click the eye icons next to the RGB, Red, and Blue channels to hide them.

10 The Channels palette, showing the setup for retouching while viewing the Green channel.

All the colors you can see on your screen are created by mixing different amounts of the three primary colors: red, green, and blue. For example, mixing red and green together produces colors such as orange, yellow, and brown.

Photoshop stores the color information of your image by keeping track of how much red, green, and blue to use for every pixel. Normally, Photoshop automatically mixes the red, green, and blue together for you and displays the result. There is, however, a way to view the individual colors separately, before they are mixed, using what are called color channels. To view the different channels of an image, go to the Window menu and select Channels. (The Channels palette will display.) You will see (for a normal color image) four channels: one called RGB, which contains the mixture of all three colors; and one each for Red, Green, and Blue, which contains just the information about how much red, green, or blue is used at a specific spot.

You can view one channel at a time by clicking it in the Channels palette. Color channels can prove very useful for retouching because, when viewed in isolation, they can highlight subtle details that might be harder to spot in the full-color image. In the retouching examples here, I use the Green channel to help visualize areas where the texture of the model's skin needs to be smoothed.

Note: There are other systems besides the three-color RGB mode for keeping track of color information in an image. The CMYK system (for cyan, magenta, yellow, and black) is commonly used when preparing images for four-color printing and has four channels of color rather than three.

9 The Channels palette in its default state.

11 Window setup for retouching.

Next, make a layer (Ctrl+Shift+N) and call it **retouching**. This layer is where you'll do the work of smoothing the skin and making it flawless. Up until now, you've been using the Healing Brush. For the next step, however, switch to the Clone Stamp tool. The Healing Brush is great for creating repairs without disturbing texture and tone. At this stage, however, you *want* to disturb the texture and tone. That is why you will be using the Clone Stamp to smooth and even out the skin. After you've selected the Clone Stamp tool, go to the Options settings and select an Opacity setting of between 20% and 30%. Also, make sure the Use All Layers option is checked. The basic approach is to use the Clone Stamp like an air-brush. For open areas such as the forehead, use a large brush size of about 100 pixels, going down to a smaller 60-pixel brush for more detailed work.

Working in the Green channel window, clone onto areas that need smooth-ing from adjacent areas of similar surface texture and color tone. This requires a bit of practice until you get the "feel" of it, but it basically comes down to blending the tones and smoothing the texture—all the textures and tones need to match and smoothly blend together. Remember, you are creating a layer that will be superimposed over the original, so don't be afraid of being too heavy handed. You will need to push some pixels around (be nice) to get the desired results. This will become second nature at some point, but for now just think "smooth, blended, and polished." When you're done, you'll have a layer of perfect smoothness that you can then blend back with your original layer to get the desired effect. Don't forget the neck area as well.

One of the great challenges, and most frequently asked questions, has to do with figuring out from where to clone. Looking at the image through the Green channel enables you to concentrate more on tone than color. Find a clean area of skin with the same tone of gray and use this as your cloning source.

When you've smoothed out all the rough spots, you can look at your retouching layer by itself to see what areas you've retouched and also what parts you may have missed. You should have a layer that looks something like Image 12.

Looking at the image now, you may feel it's flat or overdone. Well, you're right; it is! But don't worry—you aren't done quite yet. The trick is to get back some of the skin's original texture while retaining the smoothness you have just created. Close the new window showing the Green channel and go to the color one. In the Layers palette, select your retouching layer and change its Opacity to 55%. Now you have skin texture back, with even tone. (Yes, you can have your cake and eat it too!) The difference is subtle, but subtlety is exactly what reality retouching is all about. As you can see from Image 13, cutting back that bit of texture makes it look like flawless real skin, not digitally smoothed skin.

PIXEL MEASUREMENTS

Throughout this chapter, you will encounter various pixel dimensions for things such as brush size and feathering of selections. These dimensions are based on the 300 dots per inch (dpi) resolution of the example images. If you are working on higher- or lower-resolution images, you must scale these example pixel dimensions up or down accordingly.

12   The retouching layer by itself, showing the areas retouched.

Before Retouching.   Retouching 100%   Retouching 55%

13   The effect of changing the opacity of the retouching layer.

Perfect Eyebrows

Eyebrows! I do more work on eyebrows than you could possibly imagine. They are extremely important because they frame the eyes and convey so much of a face's expression. Unruly, misshapen, fuzzy, or thin brows can really detract from the appearance of an image. Unfortunately, because real eyebrows are almost never perfect, they usually have to be fixed in Photoshop. In this case, the brows were a little "unruly," and the art director wanted me to clean them up and change the shape a bit.

14   The eyebrows before and after retouching.

To achieve this sharper, cleaner, more-finished brow, begin by removing stray hairs with the Healing Brush. Next, use your Lasso tool (L key) to grab a piece of skin from above the brow (see Image 15). Feather your selection by 4 pixels and copy the area, including all the retouch work, using the Copy Merged command (Shift+Ctrl+C). Next, paste the selection into a new layer and use the Move tool (letter V) to move it to cover unwanted brow, as shown in Image 15.

Deselect (Ctrl+D) and soften the edges of your copied skin area using the Eraser tool (brush size 60) at 50% Opacity. You can see that the top of the brow line is much cleaner now, and you've achieved it without disturbing the skin texture.

Continue this process across the entire top of the eyebrow to make a clean, finished brow.

15 Selecting a piece of skin above the brow and covering the unwanted brow
    (removing stray eyebrow hairs).

A Little Dentistry

Next, we whiten the teeth. This is a simple thing, but it makes the image much more attractive. First choose your Magic Wand tool (letter W), set the Tolerance to 25, and click the teeth to establish an initial selection. Next, hold down the Shift key and continue clicking areas of teeth that were not included in the initial selection, until all the teeth are part of the selection.

16   The selection for whitening the teeth.

To refine your selection, go to Quick Mask mode (letter Q) and use your Paintbrush (letter B) tool to modify the mask. Remember, in Quick Mask mode, painting in white removes masking from an area, adding it to your selection, whereas painting in black adds in masking, removing areas from your selection.

Now that you have a refined mask, feather the selection radius by 4 pixels (Select > Feather) to give a nice blended edge.

Next, use the Levels control to adjust the whiteness of the teeth. Click the model copy layer to activate it, and then open the Levels dialog box by adding an adjustment layer (Layer > New Adjustment Layer > Levels), and move the middle slider to the left a bit. Different amounts of whitening are called for in every image, so use your own judgment and experiment until it looks right to you.

17   The quick mask of the selected teeth.

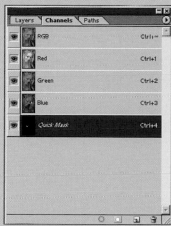

18   The Channels palette in Quick Mask mode.

19   Using the Levels control to whiten the teeth.

20   Before and after whitening the teeth.

Happenin' Hair

All right, now for one of my specialties...*hair*! As is often the case, I have some areas that need hair added, and others that need hair removed. Let's start with the right side, where I am going to pop the model out of the background, removing some hair and part of the shoulder in the process. The hardest part of removing this background will be to keep the eyelashes intact, because they stick out past the edge of the model's face and are overlapping into the area I need to remove. When you attempt this, make sure you are on the model copy layer. Then, begin by selecting large areas of the background with the Magic Wand. After you've gotten most of the background selected, begin refining the mask in Quick Mask mode by using a brush to clean up and define the edges that delineate the model from the background. Good masks are the key to getting good edges! The longer you spend in this mode refining the mask, the less work you'll have later on. Good masks are your friends!

After you've finished your mask, exit Quick Mask mode and feather the selection by 2. Then save your painstakingly created selection. To do this, click the layer mask icon at the bottom of the Layers palette. This creates a layer mask from the selection. After you have converted your selection to a layer mask, it will appear as a new alpha channel in the Channels palette. This alpha channel of your selection enables you to further refine your mask in the subsequent steps. Deselect the active selection, open the Channels palette, and click the alpha channel you just created. This turns off all the color, leaving you with a black-and-white silhouette of your mask. Any bits and pieces you may have missed will now be easily visible, and you'll be able to go in with a white paintbrush and eliminate them. Also, because you feathered the edge, you'll want to go back and cut-in the mask around the eyelashes with a small, fairly hard-edged paintbrush.

After you have perfected your mask, it's time to pop the model out of the background. Turn the RGB channel back on by clicking it in the Channels palette. This activates and makes visible all the RGB color channels, and deactivates and hides the alpha channel with your mask in it. The Channels palette should now look like Image 24.

21   The quick mask for the hair. Note that the quick mask color is set to blue.

22   The Save Selection dialog box.

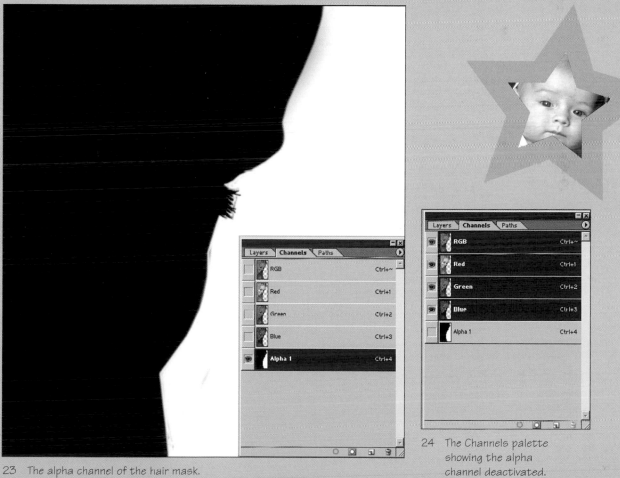

23   The alpha channel of the hair mask.

24   The Channels palette showing the alpha channel deactivated.

Next you need to turn your mask back into a selection. Ctrl+click the alpha channel you created; marching ants outlining your selection should appear in the image. Make sure your bottom "original" layer is hidden, activate your model copy layer by clicking it, and press the backspace key. Voilá, the background disappears (see Image 25)! You may still need to go in and refine those lashes one more time, but everything else should be pretty good right at this point.

Retouching hair is tricky because you can't clone it, and healing it only works in small areas. So here is my secret: I never retouch hair. I only copy, paste, and transform. That's the only way I have found to keep the texture of the hair from getting muddy. In this example, the first thing you are going to do is crop the image down. You need plenty of room on the right for type anyway, and cropping will also leave you with less hair to fill in.

After you've cropped the image, you really only have a corner to deal with. By luck of the draw, you also have one very nice piece of blonde hair that looks like a good candidate for the copy/paste/transform technique. Select that piece using the lasso, feather it by 5, and then use Copy > Paste (Ctrl+C and Ctrl+V, respectively) to make a copy and paste it back into the file as a new layer.

Now just move the pasted hair over to the left. Then, using the Free Transform command (Ctrl+T), pull up and out on the upper-left corner and rotate the selection slightly counterclockwise. The idea is to match the way the hair is falling. After feathering out the edges with a soft brush, the hair transplant should be virtually undetectable if done properly.

ADJUSTMENT LAYERS

Always use adjustment layers to make these kinds of corrections; that way you don't alter any valuable pixels. If you don't use an adjustment layer, you lose the flexibility to change your mind later. With adjustment layers, you can keep playing with the settings without making any changes to any of the pixels.

Adjustment layers will become your friends. The great thing about changing things with adjustment layers is that if the art director comes back and says "No, it needs to be purple," you already have your selection, and all you have to do is double-click to bring the dialog box back up. This proves very useful given how often art directors change their minds!

25 After deleting the masked-out hair

26 The selection of hair to copy and paste in.

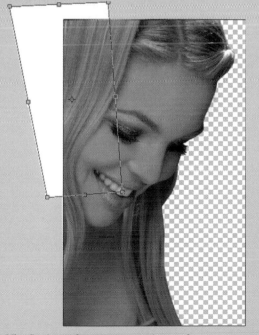

27 The hair after pasting and transforming.

Overall Look and Feel

Now that all the retouched elements are in place, you need to take a final look at the overall appearance of the image. The image at this point looks a little flat and a little dark, so you're going to use an adjustment layer to adjust the curves. First, make sure you are on the top layer of your document so that the adjustment layer will affect all the layers below. Then make an adjustment layer for the curves (Layer > New Adjustment Layer > Curves).

Place the cursor over the image and click the image where you think the tones look flat; you will see a small circle appear on the line in the dialog box. This will give you an idea of where to grab the bar. Ctrl+click to mark this spot. Pull up and down to lighten and darken. Play around here until the image looks a little more bright and punchy.

A Few Final Touches

When you have it where you like it, take a break. Step back from the computer, remove your hands from the keyboard…go look at a tree. You need to get some distance so that you can tell whether you need to do anything else. I often find things that the art director has missed. Why? Because the art director hasn't had the luxury of seeing it in this state, you have the chance to see it before anyone else, and sometimes things will just jump out at you. For instance, now that I have lightened the image considerably, I can see that the lips need to be more pink and maybe a little more intense. I remember when I shot this image the lip color was a little more vibrant. So, what can I do? Well…it's easy.

First you need to select the lips using the Polygon Lasso tool (see Image 28) and feather by 2. When you have an active selection, the selection will become a layer mask for your adjustment layer. This mask controls where the subsequent effect shows up in the image. Now add an adjustment layer for Selective Color (Layer > New Adjustment Layer > Selective Color) and adjust the reds to the desired tone. I love Selective Color adjustment because you can really change hues so subtly (see Image 29).

28 The selection around the lips.

29 Using the Selective Color options to adjust the intensity of the lip color.

All there is left to do now is paste in the background file. You need to make your canvas larger to accommodate the final proportions. Enlarge the canvas (Image > Canvas Size) to 11.5×13 inches, making sure you anchor the image to the left side and to the top (see Image 30). Now open your background file, and then copy and paste it into the final file. Make sure that the new background layer is below the model copy layer, but above your original layer.

30   Anchoring and resizing the canvas.

Your final should look like Image 31.

After you paste the background in, you may want to make a close-up inspection of how the model image blends with the sky image just to make sure that there are no rough spots that need further attention (see Image 31).

Okay, so that's it for reality retouching. Next, we'll go on to plastic surgery, which includes tips and tricks that build on the basics you've learned here.

31   Final image for reality retouch (opposite).

Plastic Surgery

If, after you've finished the work of a reality retouching, more drastic work is needed, you can move on to plastic surgery. First, do everything you can to give the image a finished appearance. I don't like to cut and paste parts until the basics are done. Also, note that you can make dramatic changes by stretching highlights and deepening shadows. This simple technique can change the shape of a cheekbone or nose. When I do my initial retouching layer, I pay close attention to the light and shadows. This becomes especially important in some lighting conditions and with older models. You can recontour someone's face by widening and lessening shadows and highlights. Pay close attention to where these shadows fall on the face, and how dark they are, and you'll be able to take years off someone's face without needing to change anything in the underlying structure.

When you open this file, it will already have a retouching layer in it. You'll clearly be able to see where the highlights and shadows have changed. I have included this so that you can see exactly what this layer looks like. In a soft yet dramatic lighting situation such as this one, there are shadows on the right side of the face that do not enhance her face structure. I blended the contours, took a little tuck in on the outer edge, and lightened the nose shadow. If you turn the layer on and off, you will see the dramatic difference it makes in her overall appearance. Just this technique alone will take years off. But wait...there's much more.

32 Before and after plastic surgery collagen injection.

Collagen Injections

With the initial retouching out of the way, it's time to move on to the surgery section of this image. Image 32 shows the before and after of reality retouch with some additional plastic surgery. Unfortunately, the model's lips were not as full as the client wanted, so we're going to work on them a bit, removing some wrinkles and enlarging them.

To work on the lips, pop them into their own layer. Create a rough selection around the lips, making sure you have a good amount of skin on the outside as well (see Image 33). Feather it at about 5, and then use the Layer via Copy command (Ctrl+J) to create a new layer from your selection. We'll do our work on the lips in this newly created layer.

The first thing to do with these lips is remove the wrinkle on the left side of the lower lip with the Healing Brush. To do this, Alt+click above the wrinkle to establish a sample point, and then click the wrinkle to heal one small section at a time. To make the lips look fuller, continue to heal the other wrinkles that go horizontally and vertically across the lip. Don't remove them all, but definitely eliminate the larger ones. Just removing these wrinkles gives the lips an appearance of more fullness.

33   The selection used for working on the lips.

34   After using the Heal Brush on the lower lip.

The next step is to adjust the shape of the lips. The shape in the original image is good but a little bit thin. To fix the problem, use the Free Transform command to stretch the layer ever so slightly.

Press Ctrl+T to launch the Free Transform command, and then, while holding down the Ctrl key, pull the center-top handle slightly up and to the left, as shown in Image 35. This action increases the smirk a little and makes the lips slightly fuller. You must reposition the lips slightly by using the arrow keys to nudge the layer. Move them back down so that the upper lip on the transformed top layer fits over the original. The following figure shows an example of the new lip superimposed over the old.

As you can see from Image 36, the upper lip stays anchored in its original position, and the bottom lip is now extending slightly below the original lower lip.

Now that you have the new lip in place, you need to become a dentist for a moment. Switch back to your original layer. Go in with the healing brush and adjust the shape of the teeth, eliminating the gaps.

35 Transforming the shape of the lips to add fullness.

36 The transformed lips superimposed over the untransformed lips.

37 Areas to work on the teeth.

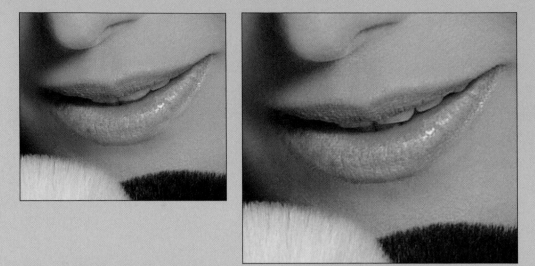

38 Before and after work on the teeth.

Next, redden the lips. Choose your Polygon Lasso tool and draw an outline of the lips. (Note that you also can use the Pen tool to make this selection.) The outline here is critical because it will define the shape of the mouth and the form of the lips, so take the time to make a really great selection, tweaking where necessary to ensure the lips have a perfect shape.

After creating your selection, feather it by 4, and then add an adjustment layer for Selective Color. Now you can begin to adjust the different colors.

I have made most of my adjustments to the red. You also can play around with the neutral. Again, having these changes in an adjustment layer means you can use a different color later if the art director requires changes.

39   The selection for adjusting lip color.

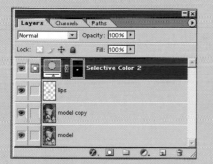

40   The Layers palette showing
     the adjustment layer for
     Selective Color.

41   Using the Selective Color options to redden the lips.

The Eye-Lift

In this next image, we are going to fix the model's right eye. Even though this model is quite young and beautiful, her right eye appears smaller than the left due to the angle of the shot. The task here is to transform it so that the eyes look more even. First begin by lassoing the area around the model's right eye (see Image 43).

42 Before and after images of a plastic surgery eye-lift.

43   Selecting and transforming the eye shape.

Feather the selection by 5, and then use the Layer via Copy command to create a new layer from your selection. Next enlarge the eye and lift the eyebrow in one transformation by pulling the upper-left corner up, and the lower-left corner out (see Image 43). After doing so, you must lower the Opacity of the layer so that you can line up the transformed layer. Lowering the Opacity enables you to see the two layers simultaneously. Line up the new layer with the original so that the bottom of the eye on both layers is in the same place. After placing it where you want it, reset the Opacity to 100%. You'll probably have some cleanup to do on the outer edge. Get your Eraser tool and, with an Opacity of 50%, use a large soft brush to work the edges. This technique creates a flawless and invisible eye-lift.

As you can see in the final retouched image, the model's right eye seems less puffy and more symmetrical with the other. Even though this difference is subtle, it gives a more fresh and appealing look.

44   The before and after of the final retouched image.

The Nose Job

This next image was initially shot for stock, and was picked up by Bombshell Studio Make-up (*bombshellstudiomakeup.com*) for their campaign. Even though the model has stunning looks at certain angles, her nose photographed unevenly. As with all of my images, I begin with the basic retouching. After the standard smoothing and cleanup, using my mental checklist as discussed earlier, I move on to the nose.

45   Before and after images of plastic surgery with a nose job.

46   Before the retouch, with notes on areas needing work.

I first assess what work needs to be done. In Image 46, I marked the parts of the nose I wanted to see fixed in the final image. On the right side of the model's nose, I must add definition, because it isn't clear where the bridge of the nose is. I also need to lessen or remove the knob on the right side of the model's nose. Finally, I will reduce the width of the nostril on the right, which will in turn lessen the nose's overall width.

In this next image, I have done all the necessary retouching to the eyebrows, lips, and skin. I also have lessened the shadow on the right side of the nose using the Dodge tool and burnt the edge, using the Burn tool, with a very small brush. The goal was to make the bridge more defined.

Now we will begin working on the right side of the model's nose. Notice that the basic retouching techniques—smoothing the skin, making the shadows less dark—have already reduced the appearance of the knob on this side, taking us halfway to the desired result.

Start on this side by copying the right half of the nose. Be sure to grab enough skin on the right side—when you transform this, you'll need the extra to cover.

Feather the selection by 5 so that you have a smooth edge, and then create a new layer from the selection.

47   After the initial retouch, before plastic surgery.

48   The selection for narrowing the nose.

49   After transforming the nose.

Next we're going to free transform the shape of the right side of the nose to lessen the overall width. We don't really need to change much. Because this is a small adjustment, make small changes until you have reached the desired effect. First drag the right side of the transform box toward the center. This action reduces the width of the nostril as well as the bridge of the nose. When the width of the bridge looks good, drag the lower-right corner of the transform box in to further reduce the size of the nostril while leaving the width of the bridge the same.

Finish off the tip of the nose by creating a new, empty layer for retouching, and then use the Clone tool to smooth out the bump on the tip.

The final step is to even out the nostrils. Because the model's head is at an angle, the nostrils appear to be two different sizes. I think the discrepancy between the two is too large and needs to be a little more even. So first

50 The selection for transforming the nostril.

select the model's right nostril, feather it by 3, and create a new layer from the selection (Ctrl+J).

Free transform this new layer by holding down the Alt key while dragging the handles to stretch and enlarge the nostril, paying close attention to angle of the nose (see Image 51).

Now move on to the other side. Transform this nostril in the same way. This time, however, just reduce the size ever so slightly.

As you can see when you compare the two images side by side in Image 52, the difference is noticeable, but it's unnoticeable if you don't have the original image as a reference point. Obviously, no one will have seen the before, so the goal is to make a great-looking image regardless of where you started.

51   The transformation to enlarge the nostril.

52 Before and after the retouch.

Xtreme Hair

I have one other item I want to show you in the plastic surgery category. It's not really plastic surgery, but more like a really big bottle of Rogaine. We're going to add *heaps* of hair!

53 The original shot before the hair extension treatment.

As you can see from Image 53, the model already has plenty of beautiful hair. However, I want to add even more to get the "extreme hair" effect I want in the final image.

54   The final image with more hair.

I work with hair using three basic moves: Copy/Paste, Transform, and Twirl. Let's start by copying chunks of hair from other source images from the shoot. Here are the three images to use as the hair transplant sources.

55 The first hair transplant source image.

56 The second hair transplant source image.

57 The third hair transplant source image.

Select chunks of hair from the source images that will more or less match the underlying hair in the target and fill out the shape and size desired. In addition to the size and shape, look specifically at the lighting and color tone. For example, notice the blue light hitting the model around the hairline—you want to make sure that all the hair emanating from this area has the same bluish cast. (Note that you also can use this technique by copying from within the same image if you don't have other sources to use.)

Believe it or not, this seemingly painstaking process is very forgiving. When you feather the edges of the pasted selections, no one will really be able to tell where one chunk starts and the other stops.

Image 58 shows a shot of the selection from the first source image. I grab as much hair as possible from this shot because it will make up for a lot of missing pieces in the original image. Also, it's nice to get a lot of coverage from one piece because it gives me less cleanup work to do.

58 The selection of the first chunk of hair for copying.

First, duplicate your background layer and turn the bottom one off. Then, extend your canvas (Image > Canvas Size) so that you have room to work. Anchor the image to the right side and create extra space on the left. Using the Eyedropper tool, sample the color from the existing background, and fill in the new background space using the Paint Bucket.

59 The target image with the first chunk of copied hair pasted in.

After copying and pasting the selected hair into your file, you should have something that looks like Image 59. Next you are going to copy a chunk for the top portion of the hair from the second source image and paste it into the file as well.

60   The target image with the second chunk of hair pasted in.

As you can see from Image 60, this is not far off from where you want to be eventually. Now you paste one more piece from the third source file and begin the transforms and twirls.

61   The target image with the third chunk of hair pasted in.

Now you twirl the ends of the hair to better match the existing hair and give it a softer, more fluid effect. Using the Lasso, grab just the parts that you want to change. Then use the Twirl filter (Filter > Distort > Twirl) to add a slight swirl effect to the selected hair (see Images 62 and 63).

62   The image after some initial twirling, showing a selection for twirling.

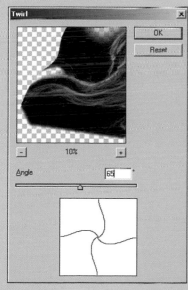

63   The Twirl dialog box.

Play with the Angle slider until the flow feels like that of the other pieces in the image.

Your initial selection is key to how your final effect will appear. If you grab a larger chunk of the same piece, you get a different effect when you twirl.

The last step is to free transform the shape of each piece you have pasted in. Stretch, pull, and move the pasted fragment until it blends in with the flow of the original hair. You're not going for perfection, because you will touch up in the next step. Instead, try to make the overall direction orientation match the rest of the hair in the image. Use your original as the guide to what the direction should be (see Image 64). Repeat this process for each of the layers containing the fragments you have pasted in.

For final touch up, use the Erase tool to blend each piece into the background. Erase around the edges of your pasted-in piece until you find places where the new hairs match up with those in the original hair layer below.

64　Transforming the pasted fragment to fit.

Fantasy Retouching

Fantasy retouching is my favorite kind of retouching. It's basically the same technique as the reality retouching except that it is designed to give a more obviously enhanced, "painted-on" look. Whereas a reality retouch will go undetected if done well, a fantasy retouch will be noticeable to all but the most casual observers. Because fantasy retouching often goes hand in hand with plastic surgery, I begin this section with an image that combines fantasy retouching with a fair bit of plastic surgery.

Yummy Skin and Body Sculpting

I refer to this style of heavily retouched skin as "yummy skin." When a client asks for "yummy skin," I know that texture is not important and that the photograph is supposed to have a painted quality when it's finished.

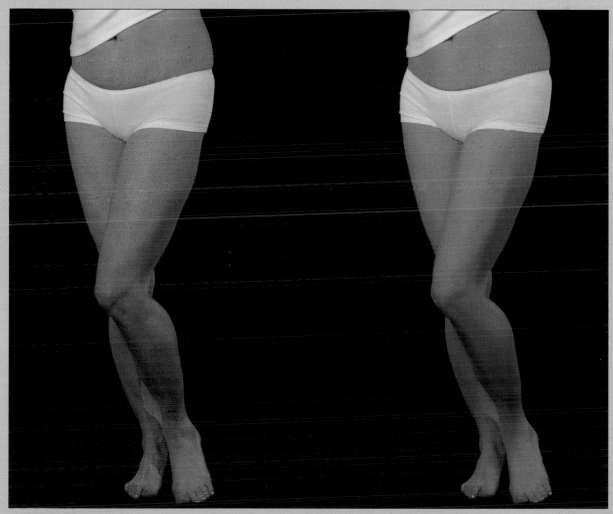

65   Before and after the skin retouching, with the retouch layer at 90% Opacity.

Having read the preceding section on reality retouching, you will already know the techniques used to accomplish this initial step. The only differences for a "fantasy" retouch are that the Opacity is set to 90% on the retouch layer rather than 30% to 60% and that broader retouch strokes are used over larger areas of skin.

As you can see from Image 65, a dramatic difference has been achieved with retouching alone. Now let's nip and tuck.

Nip and Tuck

You can give a little more definition to the model's waist in two ways. First copy a portion of the buttocks and create a new layer from the selection. Then use the Spherize filter (Filter > Distort > Spherize). This pushes the arch out to the right a little (see Image 66). You may need to erase around the edges of your selection to blend the transformed area when the filter is complete.

Now add more curvature to the waistline by using the Clone Stamp tool, with the Use All Layers option checked, on this same layer and carefully changing the shape. Use the tool to clone background over the unwanted areas, cutting-in the skin with the black background and carefully changing the shape (see Image 67). Make sure to analyze the edge you are working on, and use the right brush hardness accordingly.

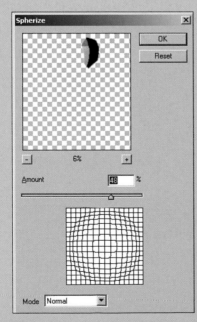

66   Using the Spherize filter.

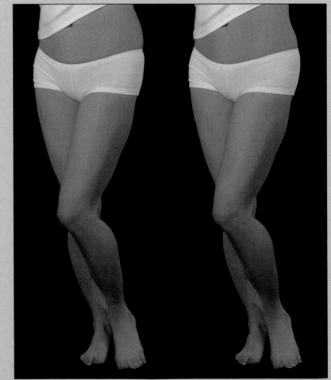

67   After spherizing and cutting in the waistline.

The next step is to narrow the width of the waist. What are we going for here? Well it's pretty much up to you. I like curves in women—I have a few myself—and so my preference is for a more curvaceous silhouette.

To start, grab a chunk of the left side with the Polygon Lasso. Then feather by 2 and create a new layer from your selection.

The Shear filter is very handy for adding slight curves to just about anything. I especially love this tool for the waistline. We are going to distort this section of the waist so that it is more indented, giving it a little bit more curve and shape. Use the Shear filter (Filter > Distort > Shear) by dragging the center of the line slightly to the left, adding curvature to the waistline.

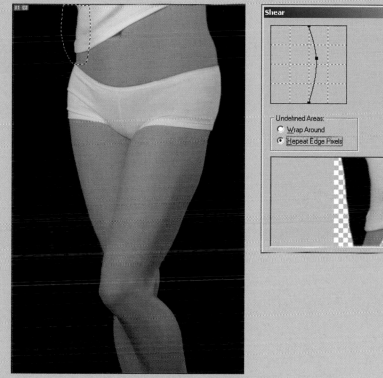

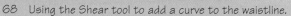
68 Using the Shear tool to add a curve to the waistline.

So here is where we're at now.

As you can see from Image 69, the difference is quite dramatic. We have made a big difference in just a few quick moves.

At this point, I Save and then Save As under a new filename. I keep many different versions of my files, creating a new one under a different name any time I flatten something or make a change I may need to reverse someday. Because you are going to flatten the image, this is a good place to begin on another copy of the file.

Defining the Legs

Now define the legs even more by dodging and burning. Use the Dodge and Burn tool to create more muscle definition on the thigh and calves. This will give the leg a sleeker look. You must make sure your image is flat before you do this, because you want the Burn/Dodge tool to be operating on all

69   After shearing the left side of the waistline.

your work to this point. Flatten (Layer > Flatten Image), and then make a duplicate of your main layer as backup. Now, go to your top layer and begin burning and dodging the highlights and shadows with the Burn/Dodge tool to create more muscle definition (see Image 70).

The reason a copy layer is so important is that, after you're done dodging and burning, you may take a look and realize that you did a little too much here and there. You can easily remedy this by using the Eraser tool on the top layer. By altering the Opacity to adjust the intensity of any of the dodging and burning effects you have just done, you can get things just right.

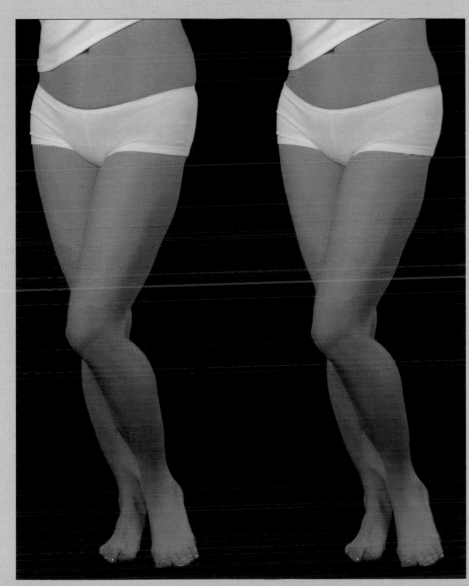

70   After burning and dodging the leg muscles.

A few last things are bothering me. First is the dip at the top of the right thigh.

Grab a piece of the upper thigh, feather by 2, and create a new layer from the selection. Free transform the selection by pulling up and out on its upper-right corner. You need to rotate the selection a little counterclockwise to make it match up. For final cleanup, touch up the edge of your selection with a soft brush.

71 Transforming the shape of the back of the thigh.

The left side of the waist needs some work; I don't think it curves in quite enough. I will again grab a chunk of the waist and use the Shear tool as seen in Image 72.

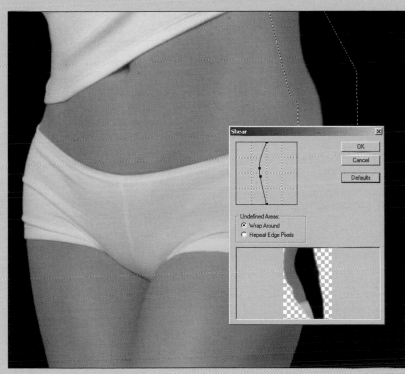

72 Shearing the right side of the waistline.

You can grab the bar at different points to make just the right curve and narrow her waist a bit. Again there should be minimal cleanup after this step.

73   Before and after of the fantasy retouch.

As you can see from image 73, all of these small changes make a big difference in the overall shape of the body.

The secret behind what I refer to as fantasy retouching is the "painterly" approach to the retouching itself, using long brush strokes with the Clone Stamp tool. Because we are retouching on a Caucasian model, we also can use the Green channel to our benefit when working.

Overall, the important thing to remember is that you will be blending tones while doing large, flowing strokes. As opposed to reality retouching, where you want to leave detail in the image, with fantasy retouching you are obliterating the detail and going for smooth and "yummy" skin that looks like it would be incredibly sleek and soft to the touch.

This chapter provides one more image from start to finish to give you another example of the fantasy retouching style.

L'amour

Quite a lot has actually gone into this image. This section covers the major steps so that you can get an idea of the workflow and the order in which things were done. In this part, I also include information on how I created her surroundings—even though this information goes beyond the "retouching" focus of this chapter.

74   Completed "L'amour" shot.

75   Before the retouching.

Star Curtain

I began by putting the stars into the background. In preparation for this, I took a shot of the set before we began shooting the model.

Using the Marquee, select a group of stars from the shot of the background and copy them. Then, in your main image, use the Magic Wand to select the background area where you'll be inserting the extra stars. Use the Paste Into command (Shift+Ctrl+V) to paste the copied stars into the background area you have selected. Finally, free transform what you've inserted so that the stars follow the pattern of their preexisting neighbors.

Repeat the star copying and pasting all the way across until you have created a curtain along the back (see Image 78). I like to create a layer set (Layer > New > Layer Set) for these parts just because it's easier to work with a file when things are organized as much as possible (see Image 79). This will complete your background for the moment.

76   Selection of stars to copy

77   Selection of background area to paste into.

78   Two steps showing the pasting and transforming of stars in the background

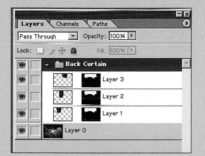

79   Separate folder for
     background layers.

On every job I do, I always photograph the set alone. Even if it's just a gray backdrop I shoot a picture of it. I do this because I never know when I'll need to extend something. Suppose, for instance, that someone needs a billboard and needs a lot more background to the right or left. With the set shot alone, I can create extra space more easily without having to get rid of the subject first.

Retouching

Now it's time to begin retouching. Begin as you did at the start of this chapter, by opening two views: your normal window, which shows the full-color image; and a Green channel window, which shows only the grayscale view of the image's Green channel (see Image 80). Your Channels palette should look like Image 81.

80 Using a view of the Green channel to retouch.

81 The Channels palette with the Green channel on.

82 During the blending process using in the Green channel.

Image 82 shows the retouching in progress. Really work on creating even blends from tone to tone. I find that if I click and drag in medium strokes, I can create a beautiful and flawless skin tone. The shadows and highlights can also be worked with at this stage to create more definition in the face. To see the actual work you've done, view the retouching layer in isolation. This will give you a look at the areas you've retouched and make it easier to see whether you may have missed something.

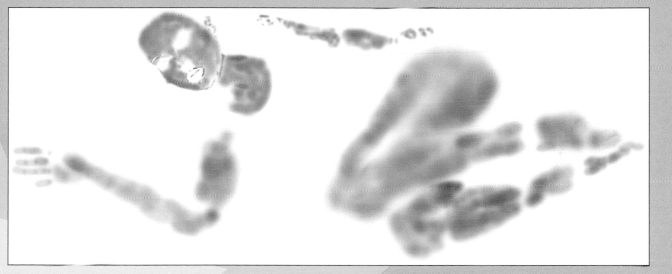

83 The retouching layer viewed in isolation.

After you have retouched the model's skin. The next thing to do is fix the eye makeup. Notice, on the right eye, the prominence of the pearlescent highlight of the eye shadow. I want to make the left eye just as pearly and shiny.

84 Selection of the eye shadow.

To copy the highlight area from the right eye, make a selection using the Lasso and feather the selection by about 10 (see Image 84). Copy the selection into a new layer, and then flip it horizontally and move it over the brow bone of the left eye. Adjust the pasted eye shadow using the Free Transform command to fit it into its new space.

85   Pasting and transforming the eye shadow.

By turning on and off the layer you just created, you can check your work, and hopefully see that the result is much more even than the original.

86   Before and after duplicating the eye shadow.

Now it's time to do some dental work. Begin by smoothing the teeth and blending the highlights using the Clone Stamp tool. Then select the leftmost tooth and create a new layer from your selection.

Move and transform the pasted tooth to fit into the empty space on the right side. Use the Levels command, moving the middle slider to the right, to bring down the overall brightness of the tooth (see Image 88). Go back in with your Clone Stamp to touch up the shape for a more uniform look (see Image 89).

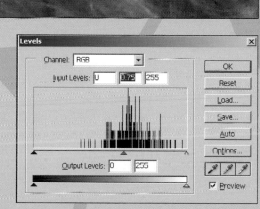

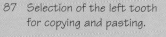
87 Selection of the left tooth for copying and pasting.

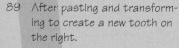
88 Using the Levels command to darken the tooth.

89 After pasting and transforming to create a new tooth on the right.

One other thing that makes the teeth look less straight is that the big white highlight is only on the right tooth. If you copy, paste and blend that highlight on the left tooth as well; this makes the teeth appear more even (see Image 90).

Image 91 shows the current state of the Layers palette at this point.

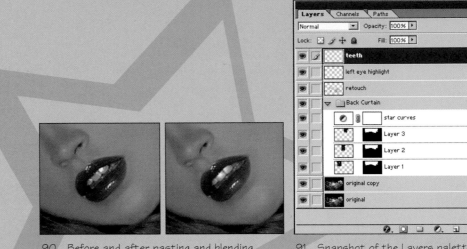

90 Before and after pasting and blending the highlights on the teeth.

91 Snapshot of the Layers palette at this point.

As a final step, before working on the image as a whole, lighten the eyebrows a bit.

92 The selection for lightening the eyebrows.

93 Using the Selective Color options to lighten the eyebrows.

First select the eyebrows and feather them by 5. Then use an adjustment layer for Selective Color to go in and lighten the blacks. This way you leave the light and midtone areas untouched and simply adjust the dark parts of the brow to be a bit lighter.

As you can see from Image 94, the eyebrow adjustment is subtle but just softens her noticeably.

94   Before and after lightening the eyebrows.

Final Enhancements

For some final adjustments, work the light and shadows with the Dodge and Burn tool. These are very subtle yet very powerful tools.

94   Before and after dodging and burning to change light and shadows.

It looks as if I have adjusted the whole image (see Image 94); in actuality, however, I just dodged and burned key areas. I significantly lightened the hair without changing any of the other tones. I also burned in the liner around her eyes, her lipstick, and under her chin, but the eyebrows remain light. I love this tool. It can really transform an image because it's like painting with light.

Warped Surroundings

The warped surroundings are all that's left to be created to finish off the image. First make a selection around the model, feather it by 50, and then create a new layer from your selection.

95   A layer without the model.

The result should be a layer that looks something like Image 95. Next, I used a KPT5 filter called Radwarp, from Corel (see Image 96). This filter does a great job of warping images—something that would take many different native Photoshop filters to create.

You can see my settings in Image 96. I play with this until I have the feel I'm looking for.

You should get a layer that looks something like Image 97.

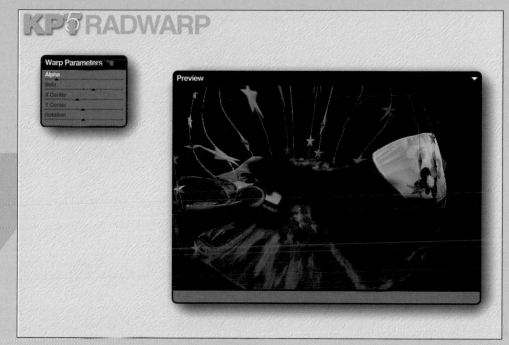

KP5 RADWARP

96   Using the KPT5 Radwarp filter.

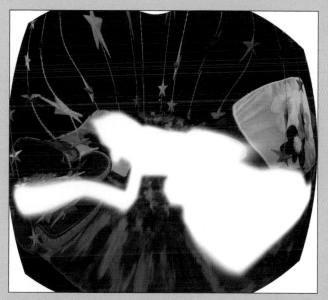

97   After the warp.

Notice how the warped image no longer covers the entire area; warping it has made it smaller. You need to transform it and stretch it to fit the entire area again. At this point, your image should look like something along the lines of Image 98.

98 The original layer under the warped layer.

Okay, now what? Well, you need to combine the two backgrounds into one. The easiest way to do that is to lower the Opacity of the new warped layer to see where you need to blend and erase to make it work with the original background.

99 Lowering the Opacity to see the layer underneath.

This gives you some idea of what needs to be done. You need to erase the layer where it overlaps the model, as well as in other key areas, such as the pink fur, that you may want to retain from the original.

To get back the original background, carefully erase between the star curtains to reveal the original pink fur. This is a time-consuming part; it takes patience, and you may have to go back if you make a mistake. Make sure during this process that you keep putting the Opacity back to 100% so that you can see how the blending and erasing are looking in the final composite (see Image 100).

100   Erasing the warped layer.

After you have done this, you should end up with something like Image 101.

101   After uncovering the background layer.

My final step is to flatten the image and add a little bit of blur. Everything is a little too sharp, and I think adding blur will give it a more dreamy quality. Open the History palette (Window > History) and make a new snapshot on the History palette by selecting New Snapshot from the History palette's drop-down menu. Name the snapshot **Final**. Then run the Blur filter—I used KPT5 Blurrr filter, and chose the Gaussian Weave setting because it gives that small crosshatch effect I was looking for (see Image 102).

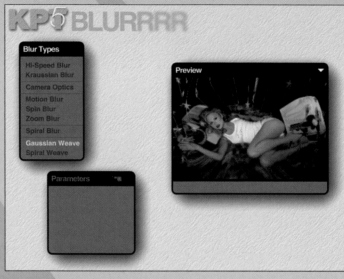

102   Using the KTP5 Blurrr filter.

103   The History palette, showing snapshots used for the History Brush.

Make another new snapshot on the History palette and name it **Blur**. Then use the Step Backward menu command to step back one step in your History palette. Click in the box to the left of your Blur snapshot to activate it as the source for the History Brush (see Image 103), and choose the History Brush from your Tool palette.

Now you can begin to paint with the blurred image, adding blur into the image according to your individual taste. By varying the brush Size, Hardness, and Opacity of the History Brush, you can vary the amount and intensity of blur that gets added in. This is very much a thing of individual taste, so it's up to you where to use it and with how much intensity.

Image 104 shows the final image. I hope that breaking this down has given you an idea how to achieve something like this in your own work. Arriving at this image has definitely required a lot of steps, but the end result doesn't "look" like it.

104   Final image.

Where We Are

You have learned the degrees of retouching from reality to fantasy. Now you are going to see some of these skills put into action. In the next three chapters, I present three images and discuss what went into their creation. I hope what you have learned in this chapter adds to your repertoire of retouching and reconstruction techniques, and I hope the next few chapters inspire you to create fantastic images of your own.

Chapter 7

Digital Statuette

I find my thoughts meandering toward joyful, gleaming. Oscar was the name, and kudos was the game. Or was her name Emmy? Six of one half a dozen of another, I end up at the same crossroads. Grab a magic wand and come along as we cast a spell to change flesh into molten metal and bring happy shiny statues to the high-tech elite.

The final product.

When *PEI* asked me to design and photograph the cover for their "2001 2Cool Awards" issue, I was thrilled. Luckily, I was given the rare luxury of unfettered creative freedom to come up with the concept for the project and to bring that vision to full completion. I decided to incorporate the project into a stock shoot I already had on the schedule. With editorial, you are often on tight deadlines; such was the case for this assignment as well.

Conception

As soon as I hung up the phone with *PEI*, I began to ponder how best to sum up their 2Cool award in one single image. The image, in this case, was not only going to serve as the cover, but was also going to have to pull double-duty as the award itself—getting mounted onto a plaque with the winner's name and the division for which the prize was awarded.

The fact that the image was actually the award began a thought process. When I hear the word *award*, I think "Academy." Because I have always envied the fact that people in the entertainment industry get a chance to win one of those beautiful golden Emmy or Oscar statues, I thought it was high time the world of technology got a chance to win one of their own. So, I decided to design a human statuette!

When I called Joan Sherwood, *PEI*'s editor, to discuss the idea, everyone enthusiastically latched onto the concept for the cover. They asked me to provide a rough storyboard so that all of us would be on the same page. I sent them the following image as a mock version of what I was thinking of creating.

The elements for the storyboard image included a shot of a real statue from a building in Hollywood and a shot of the face of the model that we hired from the casting call. The statue was popped out of its background, and the model's face was flipped, superimposed on the statue, and then transformed to fit. The whole statue was given a gold tone, and the Angled Strokes filter was used to create a hand-drawn effect. Finally, a blue background was created and the halo effect was added using Eye Candy 4000's Corona filter by Alien Skin.

You will need to download chapter7.tif from the glitterguru on Photoshop web site to complete this project.

CREATIVE COMMUNICATION

My original idea for the statue was silver, as a visual pun on the "cool" theme from the 2Cool awards. During our initial discussion of the concept, however, make-up artist Cynthia Bachman advised me that gold was much prettier painted on skin than silver. Gold also seemed more in keeping with the award statuette concept, so it eventually won out over silver. Score: Make-up artists 1, visual puns 0.

1   Original storyboard for *PEI* awards issue.

2   Original statue and casting shot used to create storyboard.

PEI loved the mockup—so much they weren't sure exactly how it could be improved—and the concept was immediately given the go-ahead.

In this chapter, I provide an overview of the production process for the cover shot and get into some detailed information on the techniques used to achieve the "golden" effect you can see in the final image.

The Shoot

After getting approval for the storyboard, I sent copies to my crew in preparation for the shoot. Getting the storyboard in the hands of your team beforehand is great, because it helps people prepare and come up with creative ideas in advance. In addition, it ensures everyone comes to the job with the same vision in mind.

The next step was to create a lighting diagram for the shot. In keeping with our "Hollywood tradition" theme, I decided to go for a dramatic 1940's film noir look. The lighting setup consisted of just two lights: an open head with a medium grid spot as my key light, and another open head behind and below the model with an amber gel.

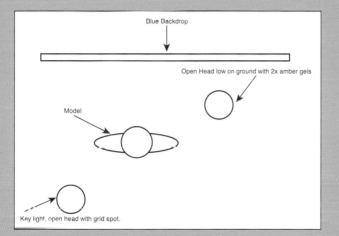

3   Lighting diagram for digital statuette shoot.

There wasn't a large budget for props and costumes, so we couldn't have a dress made for the shoot. Instead, we draped fabric that we picked up at our local fabric store. I wanted a metallic finish to the fabric, something that when draped looked like metal. The only prop we needed was the 2 for our statuette to hold. We attempted to rent a 2, but—amazing as it may seem— were unable to find a large gold 2 for rent anywhere! Falling back to plan B, my stylist Stacey Anne and I designed the 2, which she then had made by a local prop house. It's important to have an element such as this be as close as possible to what you want the final fabric to look like. Because we were short on time and budget for this job, the metallic finish on this made things go faster in post.

Make-up artist Cynthia Bachman covered the model in golden body paint and sprayed her with glitter. Knowing that a lot of retouching was going to happen, we planned for the make-up to be only a starting point, providing as much sheen as possible to build on. Eric Fox built the wig and painted it gold with spray paint.

I knew this shot was going to be heavy on the digital side, so my main focus was getting the body position perfect and making sure that the skin, fabric, and hair were picking up the metallic quality that I would need to work with later in the imaging process.

4   Cynthia Bachman, creator of Bombshell Studio
    Make-Up, begins the transformation.

5   Photo assistant extraordinaire Steve De Furio helps
    get the model's position just right.

Creating Metallic Skin and Hair

When you open up the raw image, you can see that the imperfections on the skin are really prominent. This is because the gold makeup brings out every bump and hair in glorious shiny detail. Obviously, there is a lot of work to be done smoothing the skin out before we get the metallic look we're going for, so we'll need to blend the skin. When I say "blend," what I mean is that you need to push around the pixels. Imagine you're making a smoothie (yum). You put in the raw ingredients—a chunk of banana, some chopped-up strawberries, maybe some pineapple chunks, some milk…(sounds good)—and then you turn on the blender. What do you get? A nice smooth drink. Well, we need to do the same thing here. You need to be the blender. Use long smoothing strokes; you want to blur all those little marks and blemishes and make them more smooth and yummy. Begin working on this like any other image by doing a fantasy retouch using the techniques from Chapter 6, "Beauty Retouching." In this case, the Green channel, as explained in Chapter 6, is very helpful in showing you these imperfections. Really concentrate on smoothness, using the Clone tool like a palette knife on clay. You literally need to create a new texture for the skin as liquid as glass.

We are going to do some heavy "painting" to achieve this smoothly blended skin tone. Use your Clone tool to spread highlights or eliminate unwanted shadows. Basically, think of the original skin as a guide to color, highlight, and shadow. The rest is up to your artistic interpretation. You have the ability to change the way light hits the surface of the skin. You also have the ability to make highlights longer and shadows deeper, which enables you to create very powerful effects. By stretching a highlight, you can make a thigh appear longer and sleeker. By deepening a shadow, you can make a cheekbone appear more prominent. You can change the angle of that cheekbone by bringing the end of a shadow up rather than down. This concept is *very* important for you to understand. It will change the way in which you think about retouching. When you realize that you can use highlights and shadows to reconstruct just about anything, you will have a very potent tool at your fingertips.

6　Original unretouched image.

7　Using a view of the Green channel to begin the smoothing/retouching process.

8　Showing the progression of the smoothing/retouching process, using a view of the Green channel.

Let's talk a little about filters for a second. I generally don't like them, because people tend to use them as a substitute for creativity—throwing filters at an image in an attempt to make it look like "digital art." In my opinion, you should use filters as tools to get you to the final product you are envisioning, rather than as the main focus of the final product itself. That said, some filters are fantastic time savers, and the effects in this particular image lent themselves well to filter use. I mention a few filters in this book, but that's because they save you time, and that saves your client money. In my work, that is key to keeping my clients coming back.

9   Settings used for the Glare filter.

The hair in the original image doesn't convey the impression of smoothness needed for the final image. We want to try to give it a more plastic/metallic feeling and get rid of some of the detail. Make a selection around just the hair and copy and paste it onto a new layer.

I really needed to enhance the metallic highlights in the hair, so I used a filter called Glare by Flaming Pear. Of the few filters I do use, this is one of my favorites (because of its versatility). It works on several parts of the image simultaneously, on highlights, and on color tone.

After applying the filter, we still needed to make the hair look more fluid and less real. We used the Smudge tool from the Tool palette and set it to a Pressure of 12%. Then we used a brush about half the size of each loop of hair and smeared it the direction of the hair strands. Keep repeating this technique until you have achieved the desired effect. You can use the Smudge tool to create flow. You need to give this hair the feeling of spun gold. Think in terms of highlights and shadows, not retouching. You need to smooth and blend to create this new texture.

Background Effects

We knew from the storyboard that the background would be blue, and I had envisioned a starry night with some kind of galactic aura around the statuette. We started by creating the starry background.

Years ago you would have had to create this background by painstakingly airbrushing 10 or 20 different-size dots of various hues over and over again; or perhaps by adding noise to a layer of black, blurring it slightly, and then using a blending mode to merge it with the existing background. Now, however, in the world of filters, you can do it in a matter of seconds. The Glitterato filter by Flaming Pear enables you to create the exact star field you need, quickly and beautifully. This filter has excellent controls and sliders. By adjusting the Density, Brightness, Scale, and other options, you can create an amazing custom star field effects. You can create a simple starry night or even nebulas. It's pretty amazing.

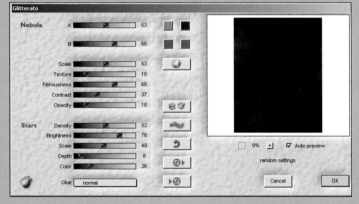

10   Settings used for the Glitterato filter.

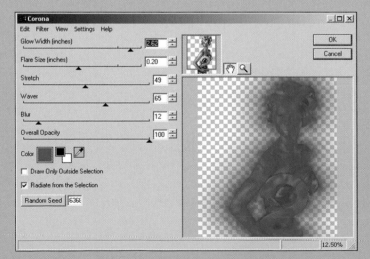

11   Settings used for the Corona filter.

12 Using the History Brush to paint back
    in the Corona effect.

Next, we created the aura around the statuette. This could have been done
by hand, but, in this case, the filter just made life easier. We started by
applying the Corona filter by Eye Candy 4000. Apply the filter and take a
snapshot by choosing New Snapshot on your History palette. Step backward
when in your History palette to remove the filter from the image. You
should see your original image again; under the Snapshots on the History
palette, however, you should also see a picture with the filter applied.

Choose your Art History Brush and click the brush icon next to the snapshot that you just created. Begin to paint the Corona back in. The Art
History Brush is great for this kind of work, because you can control exactly
how and where the Corona filter will appear in the image. You can vary the
effect by choosing different blending modes or by changing the Opacity of
the brush itself. On this image, I worked with the History Brush in a variety
of opacities. I usually start with a low Opacity, such as 15%, and begin to
paint in the Corona effect. I then work my way up to a heavier Opacity of
75%. You want to build up the layers so that you will have some subtle
areas and some more obvious area.

Final Touches

Next let's talk about the fabric of the dress. To smooth the texture on the dress, we used the Smudge tool as we did before on the hair. I like the Smudge tool because it's very "painterly" and has a different feel than the Blur tool. It's great for this type of application where you want a smooth but directional flow. Remember to pull the Smudge tool in the same direction the fabric is flowing; this will give a liquid feel to the fabric.

Now, as a final pass, take the Smudge tool and go over the highlights and shadows on the skin. Make sure you have worked the length, angle, and width of the highlights and shadows. This is the key to creating our statue of gold. This final pass with the Smudge tool gives the skin a nice polished feeling. I loved following this heavy retouch with the Smudge tool because it just finished it off and gave it a real glassy, gleaming feeling. If nothing else, this project will give you a new respect for that little Smudge tool. It's not used very much, but for this image we really worked it overtime. Here is the final product.

13   Final pass with the Smudge tool to give a really polished feeling.

14   Final image for the *PEI* "2Cool" issue.

Where We Are

As you can see, ideas for images can come from just about anywhere. In this case, a small seed of an idea grew into a magazine cover. These wacky ideas force me to think of new ways to use my trusty tools...pushing my abilities a little further with every new project. This is one of my favorite aspects of digital photography and imaging. Figuring out new ways to accomplish the task at hand is what keeps this glittery chick on her toes. Now let's move on to a tale of stars and stripes.

Chapter 8

America The Beautiful

Lying asleep in my bed, sugar plums no longer dance in my head. The colorful dreams filled with glitter that I usually see have been altered. The brightest of red, white, and blue make a kaleidoscope of shapes that soar through the heavens of my inner thoughts. Open your eyes and join me as pixels dance lightly into the shapes of stars and stripes.

You will need to download chapter8_1.tif and chapter8_2.tif from the glitterguru on Photoshop web site to complete this project.

"America the Beautiful," from my stock portfolio, was created based on an image that came to me in a dream after 9/11. It has been included in this book because it really demonstrates how, using Photoshop, you can create a great-looking final product from less-than-perfect raw materials. As you will see in this chapter, the original file used for the image is very rough, and without being imaged in Photoshop it would basically have been useless. This image also demonstrates how, in some cases, the lighting on the raw image will intentionally be different from that in the final image you are trying to create. Finally, we take the retouching methods you learned in Chapter 6, "Beauty Retouching," and really put them into overdrive—showing you the kind of tremendous transformations you can accomplish with these techniques.

The Storyboard

Whenever possible, I suggest that you create a sketch or mockup beforehand that shows the basic elements, angle of the shot, and any important makeup or lighting effects that will go into the image. Then, if you can, show this image to the people working on the shot in advance. This will enable them to arrive at the shoot better prepared.

The main shot used for this image came from a session we squeezed in after a shoot for one of my cosmetics clients. I asked the makeup artist and assistant to stay after and do this image with me. Because of the time constraints we were under, I knew we were going to have to throw things together, so I wasn't expecting "the perfect shot" to start with. I knew, however, that if I could get the right expression from the model and the right angle, this image would come to life.

I've mentioned in several other chapters that storyboards are a key factor in successfully creating an image; in this case, where time was limited, having a storyboard to work from was especially important. Storyboarding was key because it kept everyone focused on a common vision and allowed us to produce, in a short amount of time, the basic elements needed to create the final image.

Image 1 shows the storyboard that was given to the makeup artist and photo assistant before the shoot. As discussed in Chapter 2, "Preproduction," you can use any number of techniques to create your storyboard, from freehand sketches to collages of magazine cutouts. Because I'm not much of a sketch artist, I generally use my favorite tool (Photoshop) to quickly whip something together that gets across the key elements of the concept. To create this specific storyboard, I started with an image of the model I had around from a previous shoot and used the angled strokes filter that comes standard in Photoshop to make it into an illustration.

1   Starting with a simple storyboard allows you to share your vision with
    the entire team.

Keep in mind that the storyboarding process provides a great time to play
with variations on the idea. You may have a vision in your mind, but when
you actually go to put it on paper things will most likely change. The angle
you originally pictured may not work, or the idea may not be coming across
as you thought it might. Take advantage of this, and use the time you spend
storyboarding to refine the idea you've had floating around in your mind.
Remember, it's better to do your experimentation beforehand when you
have plenty of time, rather than at the shoot itself, when the clock is ticking.

In this specific case, I experimented quite a bit with different color options—did I want red and white stripes on the lips, or on the eyes? I also played with the makeup to make sure it represented the feeling I was trying to convey. I needed to graphically impart a certain idea and feeling with just a few elements. I played with a couple of different scenarios. The idea of a drop of blood coming out of her lip was one, but after seeing it on paper I decided it was too much information. I also considered putting a teardrop coming down her face, with the reflection of the flag in it. Eventually, however, I ended up deciding that having the flag firmly planted in her lip helped the image better capture the atmosphere of unease that I was trying to communicate.

The Shoot

In addition to storyboarding, it's a good idea to do a lighting diagram before your shoots. Although I like to create my diagrams in Photoshop, you can use whatever works best for you.

This lighting is very simple. The model is lit by a large softbox from above and to the left. A reflective silver backdrop close behind her completes the setup for the shot.

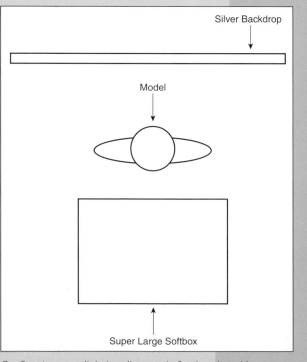

2   Setting up a lighting diagram beforehand enables you
    to concentrate on the effect you're trying to achieve.

The main reason for this lighting setup is that, although I wanted some shadows, I needed the face to be lit fairly brightly to give me enough detail to work with. In the storyboard, a dramatic lighting effect is seen where the center of the image is brightly lit but falls off sharply on each side. Had I tried to achieve this effect in my lighting setup through lighting alone, I would have ended up with a raw image that was very bright in some places, but very dark in others. This would have left me with much less visible detail to work with in the dark areas when the time came for the retouching steps.

Having enough detail in your original is key when trying to create something in Photoshop, especially for retouching. Retouching something that's in deep shadow is much more difficult than retouching something that's evenly lit. For this reason, simple lighting can be great as a starting point when you know an image is going to be really worked over and basically relit in Photoshop. Image 3 shows a photograph of the set and the actual setup—simple but effective.

3 Actual lighting setup from the shoot.

Image 4 shows the original, unretouched image. As you can see, the raw image contains *lots* of detail—obviously more than we want or need. However, this is better than not having enough detail, because it's easy to smooth out bumps, but hard to add them in. We also have the shadows basically where we want them, and these will be intensified as we change the lighting in Photoshop. As you will see in the next section, the retouching work is made easier by this lighting decision.

The makeup artist took my storyboard and, in about 10 minutes, gave me what you see here. Although he didn't have time to make it anywhere near as perfect as he normally would, I got what I needed. The lips were covered in blue lipstick, and star-shaped confetti was set down on the lips. The lips were key to making this shot a reality, so the makeup artist's work was critically important. Creating this effect in Photoshop would certainly have been possible, but it probably would never have looked as good, to my eye, as the real thing.

4 Original image.

Retouching the Model

The raw image we selected as a starting point had all the basic elements I was looking for: lighting, angle, and expression. Of these elements, expression is generally the most important thing to look for. Whereas you can tweak lighting in postproduction, and live with an angle that's not exactly what you wanted, there's no way to create a true expression. Certain frames will (hopefully) have the expression you're looking for, the expression that evokes the feeling you are trying to achieve; these will be the ones you select during the editing process.

As far as what needs to be done, pretty much every pixel will be altered—we're talking major overhaul here, not just an enhancement or embellishment. For starters, we need to address the skin texture and tone, eye makeup, and eye color. Then, the flag and its shadows need to be added and the lighting changed.

To begin with, make a working copy of your Background layer and name it model. Turn off the original Background layer, leaving it as a "just-in-case" backup, and work on the model layer from this point forward. Because we need the model's face to be white, the first step is to get rid of the skin tone. You can start by making a mask like the one in this example using Quick Mask mode (letter Q) and painting over the eyes and lips.

5   Hue/Saturation adjustment layer mask with masking mode transparency at 100%.

Then, create a new adjustment layer for Hue/Saturation (Layer > New Adjustment Layer > Hue/Saturation). Drag the Saturation slider to the left to desaturate the colors in the unmasked areas.

By desaturating first, we have less visible color to deal with in the subsequent steps. In this case, because we're going for a whitish skin tone, desaturating the colors gets us one step closer to where we ultimately want to be.

Next, reload your selection. Using the mask you just created on the Hue/Saturation adjustment layer, Ctrl-click the layer mask icon and your selection will reappear. Create a new adjustment layer for Selective Color (Layer > New Adjustment Layer > Selective Color) to change the skin tone even more.

The Selective Color adjustment is a very powerful tool, and I frequently use it when I want to "tweak" the color tone of an image. It enables you to independently adjust nine different color components of an image, all from within one dialog box. The collection of dialog boxes shows the changes made to each individual color option. I arrived at these adjustments by assessing which colors I wanted to remove. For example, skin tone has a lot of red and sometimes magenta or yellow. Therefore, we need to adjust the red to more of a cyan shade to eliminate the underlying color of the skin tone.

6   View of changes made with Hue and
    Saturation palette.

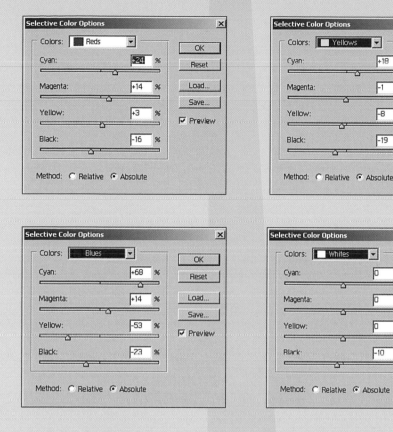

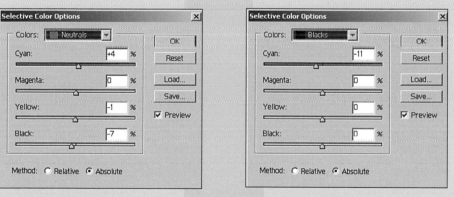

7 Changes made with the Selective Color adjustment layer.

Look at all areas of the skin, deciding which tones are the unwanted ones, and try to eliminate them using these controls. You'll find that by making adjustments to the sliders you'll be able to bring the skin tone closer to the ghostly paleness we are trying to achieve. Follow this process through all the different options in the Color menu, experimenting with how much and which colors need to be altered.

The next step is to retouch the skin.

I did this using my standard "fantasy retouch" technique as outlined in the retouching chapter. The one big change I made was with the eyebrows, removing most of the hairs and doing some "plastic surgery." I got the right eyebrow just the way I wanted it by retouching and transforming it at an angle, very much like the eyebrow we changed in Chapter 6. When I had the right eyebrow exactly the way I wanted it, I copied it, flipped it, and blended it in with the left eyebrow. Blending the copied eyebrow in with the existing eyebrow, instead of just pasting the flipped eyebrow in straight, helped to keep the two eyebrows from looking unnaturally identical. At this point, we are done with the initial retouching of the model as you can see in Image 8, so we're going to merge all the visible layers into one. Make the model layer the active layer by clicking it, and then choose Merge Visible in the Layers palette.

8   Color-adjusted images before and after initial retouch.

Adding the Flag

That same day I also photographed the flag that I would need for the final image. It's just a small, inexpensive flag, and I used tape along the backside to create a ripple effect in the fabric. The flag was photographed in the same light as the model.

9 Flag popped out of background.

LIGHTING FOR COMPOSITING

If you want things to look like they belong together in an image, the lighting needs to match. The eye is very sensitive to differences in light-ing, and viewers will subconsciously notice that something is "not right" if the angle, intensity, hue, or sharp-ness of lighting on an object differs from that of its surroundings. Obviously, the easiest way to get the lighting to match is to photograph everything under the same lighting setup. If this isn't possible—for instance, if you are adding an object to a scene that has already been shot—you need to carefully analyze the lighting in the original scene and try to re-create it in the studio.

Next, using the Mmagic Wand tool, I separated the flag from its back-ground. Then I planted it firmly in the model's bottom lip.

To complete the illusion, the shadows are critical. I have built three shadows for the flag. First are very small shadows the pole would cast on her in two places: one where it enters her lip, and the second from the pole itself onto her lip. The final shadow is from the flag itself. This is a copy of the flag layer, which is turned black by setting the Brightness and Contrast to 0. The shadow is blurred slightly with the Gaussian Blur filter, set to an Opacity of 25 percent, and then moved slightly down and to the left of the original flag. As a final touch, I used the Eraser tool to remove a bit of the shadow around the upper edge of the lip, to preserve the illusion that the lip pro-trudes and catches the light from above.

Retouching the Overall Image

At this point, the composition of the image is complete. Now is the time to go back, reassess what you've done, and do a final touch-up pass over the image.

Next we move on to the lighting adjustments. First, we want to make the model's face pop out a bit more, so we create a silhouette by darkening the left- and right-lower corners of the image around the model's face. This creates dramatic focus by slightly obscuring the unimportant information in these areas. Just select the area as shown in Image 11 and bring down the Brightness (Image > Adjustments > Brightness/Contrast), creating a deep shadow.

Leave some detail visible—we don't want complete blackness here. In the next step, we use the Melancholytron to darken this area further and we want to have some detail left to work with.

10 View of the Layers palette for flag shadows.

11 The selection used to silhouette.

The Melancholytron

Up until now, we've made some pretty dramatic changes using tools from our arsenal of retouching techniques. Now we are going to add "mood" to the image to give the final image more impact. I wanted to create a feeling of drama through the use of light and shadow. We can accomplish this using one of my favorite filters: Melancholytron, by Flaming Pear.

12   Screen grab of the Melancholytron filter dialog box.

The basic idea of the Melancholytron is that it works around the edges of an image, changing focus, brightness, and color saturation, to create vignette- or fish-eye-like effects. As suggested by the filter's name, the effect can add "mood" to an image, making it seem "somehow sad." The darkening and blurring also add an aging effect, reproducing some of the characteristics of old photographs, including edge distortions, color bleeding, vignetting, and sepia tones. The fact that these changes are applied gradually, growing more intense toward the edges of the image, tends to draw the viewer's focus to the center of an image and can heighten its overall impact. The nice thing about the variety of adjustments the filter offers is that it allows the creation of these subtle effects quickly and easily.

The Melancholytron's settings are divided into three groups. The Shape settings determine whether the effect moves out from the center in a circular, horizontal, or vertical fashion. Choosing Tall along with a clear area of 12, means that we're working out toward the left and right side, and leaving the center 12 percent of the face alone.

The Focus settings cause the areas farther from the center to get progressively more blurred and have their colors bleed. The Focus slider controls the amount of blur, and the Color Blur and CB Width settings work together to determine the intensity and width of the color bleeding. In this case, we're not going for a big "blur" effect, so the Focus setting is left at a value of 20, which keeps the blur barely noticeable. The Color Blur effect is very subtle to begin with, so fairly high settings of 54 for Color Blur and 74 for CB Width were used, although this effect is mostly hidden when the edges of the image are cast in shadow by subsequent settings.

The Color settings offer several different options for changing the color around the edge of the image. Saturation affects the hues within the original image, changing them from cool (blue) to warm (red). In this case, the high Saturation value amplifies the intensity of the red eyebrows, keeping them colorful even as the image gets darker toward the edges. The Dampen setting allows the deepening of shadows and dark areas of the image; this preserves much of the detail of an image, as well as bright colors, but makes the overall appearance more dark and moody. The Vignette slider controls the most obvious effect within this filter, overlaying the edges of the image with a gradient of the selected color (in this case black). The last slider, Sepia, causes the image to gradually have all of its color replaced with the selected color. A nice feature of the Melancholytron in this respect is the ability to gradually blend in the sepia-tone effect.

You can see how much depth and mood was added just by using this filter in Image 13. The image has changed completely, and now matches much more closely the vision I had in my mind's eye.

Keep in mind that it would be possible to create this effect in Photoshop without the use of a filter. When you get right down to it, in fact, any image or effect can be reproduced using nothing more than the Pencil tool and a lot of time. I tend to be somewhat of a purist and generally avoid using filters in much of my work. Some filters, however, are such real time savers, or give you such creative options, that they have a place in these chapters because of their value in "real-world" work where time is of the essence.

Where We Are

This image was definitely a Photoshop workout, but there is more to the creative process than just "cutting loose" with your digital toolkit: Forethought and preparation are the keys to creating your vision. I know it may seem like creating an image following a preset storyboard is rigid or somehow less creative, but quite to the contrary, this approach allows me to have *more* creative freedom. Storyboarding out what you have visualized in your mind's eye allows you to analyze all the elements you'll need to create and makes it possible to produce almost anything you can visualize. It is truly a rewarding feeling to go from a mental image through all the production steps to a final product. This process can also make you money, because clients see that you can create what you visualize.

Having a solid set of techniques under your belt, such as the different types of retouching and plastic surgery, can really pay off in a situation such as the one we were faced with in this image. With all the tools at your disposal, you have the ability to completely rework an image. Even lighting, as you saw, can be changed so that what appears in the final image is very different from the original material. This is very different from traditional photography where everything is captured at once. We are creating a photographic image with many tools other than the camera, and the production of the raw image is just the first step in what is now an infinitely flexible creative process.

13   Before and after Melancholytron.

Chapter 9

The Borg

There in my head...meandering about, ever changing into new formations as I sit and chat. Call them delusions, perhaps visions, of a skewed reality, amplified realism. Born from these episodes are these caricatures of real people. Visuals created in almost a Ouija-like trance; some unexplainable force spurs me to craft pixels into strange and fascinating things. Climb aboard our saucer-shaped ship for a trip to the outer limits of space.

You will need to download chapter9_1.tif and chapter9_2.tif from the glitterguru on Photoshop web site to complete this project.

Throughout this book I've said that when doing compositing, it's best to shoot all the elements of an image under the same lighting conditions. Sometimes, however, you will want to combine elements that weren't initially intended to be composited together. Although this is less than ideal, the capabilities of Photoshop are certainly up to the task, and having the option of using elements from a variety of sources opens up a huge range of creative options to you.

With this in mind, we're going to depart from my standard practice a bit for this chapter and discuss some techniques for working with elements that weren't shot under the same lighting conditions.

"The Borg" image we're using as this chapter's example is near and dear to my heart, because it's of my super-smart husband. Not only is he willing to put up with all of my wacky, creative endeavors, but he'll also let me re-image him into a Borg-like creature. He's such a smarty-pants that I was sure there had to be a motherboard somewhere in that head of his, so I decided to create a computerized version of him!

Initial Retouch

I lit the initial shot with one umbrella on the left, and an open head on the right with an orange gel. Looking at the original image, you can see the effect of the orange gel on the right. This "amplifies" the skin tone, because it's in the same color range as the skin, only more saturated. As you'll see, in this image the hue of the skin is going to get shifted to a cool blue. Using the orange gel enabled me to shift the color of the whole face in Photoshop later using Selective Color and get a more intense color in the area where the orange light was hitting.

The first thing I needed to do was make this much more dreamy and surreal using the fantasy retouch technique from Chapter 6, "Beauty Retouching." We're going for something that's very obviously been enhanced, kind of a special-effects look, so reality is out the door here.

Image 3 shows the results of the initial retouch. The retouching layer is done with very heavy strokes using a large-size brush, and I have paid a lot of attention to the left side. I left the upper right a little messy, because it's going to be covered up in a later step.

Looking at the retouching layer by itself will give you an idea of the painting that was done. Because we're going for a "fantasy" look, the layer will remain at 100% Opacity.

1 The original shot used in the image.

Model

Key light, open head with grid spot.

Open Head with orange gel.

2 Basic lighting setup for the Borg raw image.

3 The image after the fantasy retouching step.

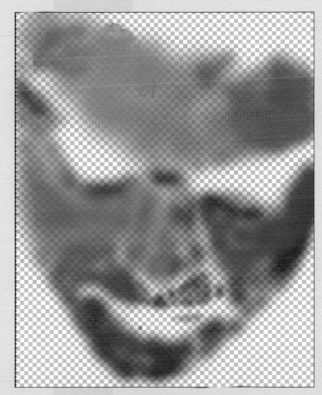

4 A view of the retouching layer.

Initial Retouch 197

Fitting the Implant

Next, we are going to get the motherboard part of the shot ready. To do this, we're going to be working with three files; the main image you already have open, a file containing a shot of the motherboard fragment, and a new file you're going to create called a *displacement map*. The motherboard image is a picture of a prop from an old shoot, and is basically a motherboard that's been intentionally bent out of shape. Shape-wise, it's in the right ballpark, but it's not exactly right. So, to give it a nicer fit, we need to use the Displace filter to make a small adjustment in the way the motherboard appears to bend.

To use this filter, you need to make a map of what you need this motherboard image to bend around. Create a new layer that is a copy of your original Background layer and retouch out the eye. I have removed the left eye so that the filter does not displace this area. My goal was to get the motherboard to flow with the natural shape of the skull, but I also wanted it to feel like an attachment or alteration, so I didn't want it to be an absolutely perfect fit around the eye. Use the Desaturate command (Image, Adjustments > Desaturate) to make this layer black and white. The final product should resemble Image 5.

Now copy and paste the motherboard into your file and place it in its final position covering the upper-right corner of the face. Load the outside selection of the motherboard by Ctrl+clicking (Cmd+clicking) the motherboard layer in the Layers palette. Next, use this selection to copy a chunk from the lower black-and-white layer. Make a new file called **map.psd**, paste this piece into the file, and save. Your map.psd file should look something like Image 6.

You've now created the black-and-white "map" that the Displace filter will use to distort the motherboard. You can now go back to your original file, deselect all (Ctrl+D), and delete the desaturated black-and-white layer used to create the map.psd file.

Next, we're going to run the Displacement filter to wrap the motherboard around the forehead.

5 The black-and-white layer used to create the displacement map.

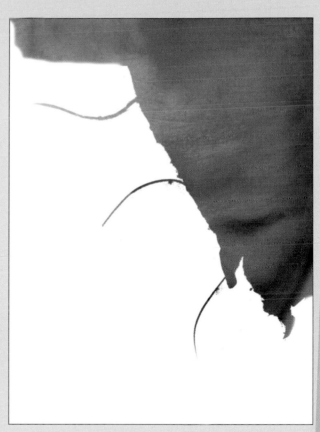

6 The map.psd file, used for the displacement map.

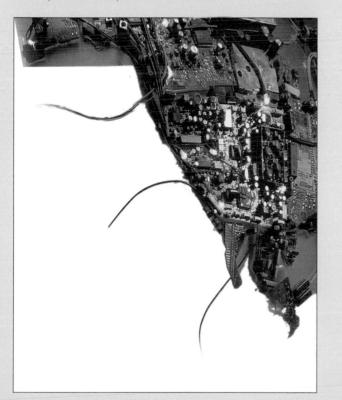

7 The motherboard image.

Displace

Horizontal Scale `50` %

Vertical Scale `50` %

Displacement Map:
- ⦿ Stretch To Fit
- ○ Tile

Undefined Areas:
- ○ Wrap Around
- ⦿ Repeat Edge Pixels

OK

Reset

8   The Displace filter dialog box.

The Displacement filter is fairly easy to use. First go back to your original motherboard file. For this example, select Filter > Distort > Displace, and in the resulting dialog box put the number 50 in both boxes as shown in Image 8. When you click OK, you will be asked to tell it which file to use to displace the image. Choose the map.psd file you just created. You can play with these ratios to cause different effects as to how the map is applied to the image.

Image 9 shows a composite of the motherboard without the Displacement filter and a composite after running the Displacement filter, cleaning the edges, and retouching. I used Luminosity as my blending mode; as you can see, the difference when applied is subtle. After the filter has been run, the motherboard is a bit shorter and more spherized. This helped give me the effect that some kind of head modification was done to the subject's brain.

To complete the implant, you need to expose some of the model's eye by removing a portion of the motherboard with a slightly feathered erase tool. (Note that if you want greater flexibility, you could also use a layer mask to create the same results.) Image 10 shows what this image should look like at this step in the process.

At this point, the basic elements are in place and we're ready to start the "finishing" work. This includes a bit of adjustment to the lighting, detailing on the eye, overall color, and some final special effects.

9   Original motherboard vs. displaced and retouched motherboard.

10   The image after completing the motherboard implant.

Lighting Adjustments

The first thing we need to address is the lighting on the motherboard. Because this element was shot under different conditions from the main image of the face, the lighting doesn't match. Specifically, the motherboard components are too bright, and the shadow of the board doesn't fall off correctly for the shape of the face. This is okay to some extent, because we've already decided to journey into "fantasy land," and the mismatch can add a desired subliminal unease to the final image. On the other hand, there are a few things that can be done to better blend the lighting conditions of the motherboard element with the face so that the mismatch is less noticeable. After you've done this, it will no longer look like the board was shot under completely different lighting conditions, but instead will look as if you added a small pinpoint spot, focused on the board, as part of your original lighting setup for the shot.

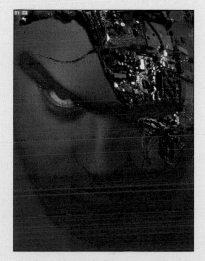

11 A quick mask illustrating the selection for the first Curves adjustment.

The first goal is to darken the overall image of the motherboard, while preserving its detail and contrast. To do this, you need to create a selection around the motherboard. To start, turn the shape of the motherboard layer into a selection by Ctrl+clicking the motherboard layer in the Layers palette. Then, enter Quick Mask mode (letter Q) and paint out part of the area under the left eye with white paint (see Image 11). By doing this, you're adding the area under the eye to your selection so that when the adjustment is made it will deepen the socket of the eye at the same time it darkens the motherboard. Next, use the Curves command (Layer > New Adjustment Layer > Curves) in an adjustment layer, bringing down the level of the mid-tones (see Image 12). This makes a minor adjustment in the mid-tones. Adjusting just the midtones leaves the bright parts bright and the black parts black, preserving details, while darkening the image as a whole.

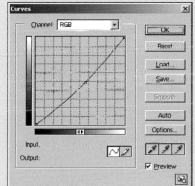

12 The Curves adjustment for the motherboard.

Next, I needed to move on to the right edge of the motherboard. As you can see, this area is brightly lit and needs to be adjusted quite a bit to match the shadow of the subject's head. To begin with, we'll make a selection, using Quick Mask mode and painting in white with a soft-edged brush where his head would begin to darken.

Then, we'll use a Curves adjustment layer to deepen the tones.

As you can see from the dialog box settings, to get the deep shadow effect, the highlights and mid-tones have both been brought down quite a bit.

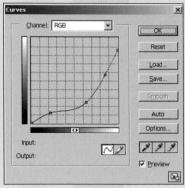

14 The settings for the second
    Curves adjustment.

13 A quick mask illustrating the selection for the
    second Curves adjustment.

Overall Color

Now, I'll move on to the overall color of the image. I've tried to go as far as I can without doing the color change because I prefer to look at the image with real skin tone as long as possible. Staying with the real skin color as long as possible helps me see more easily any problems that may arise. However, at this point, I need to see how everything will come together with the shift of tones.

To shift the overall color scheme, we're going to make a number of changes to various color palettes using the Selective Color adjustment as an adjustment layer. Images 15 through 17 show the exact changes I used.

This step has a bit of trial and error. I knew I wanted cool tones, but getting it just right took some experimentation. With the Selective Color adjustment layer done, I thought that the tones of the overall image still seemed a bit too bright. To remedy this, I added one more Curves adjustment layer to bring down the brightness of the image as a whole.

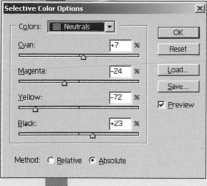

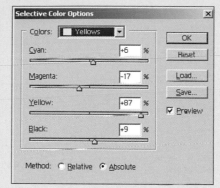

15 The Neutrals Selective Color adjustment.

16 The Yellows Selective Color adjustment.

17 The Reds Selective Color adjustment.

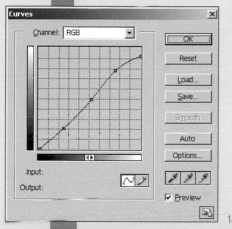

18 Final Curves adjustment.

19 The image before and after completion of the color adjustments.

Finishing Touches

Several things still need to be done, including enhancing the eye color and adding the all-important electric power! We'll start with the color of the eye.

The eye in this image is so important that we need to bring some focus to it. To do this, we use the Selective Color command, as an adjustment layer, to enhance the color of the red blood vessels and the iris. First, click the main layer to activate it. Next, using Quick Mask mode, mask out the area of the eye. Note that because the image is now blue, I have changed the color of my mask to green so that it can be more easily seen (see Image 20). To finish this step, exit Quick Mask mode, and then run the Selective Color command as an adjustment layer.

Images 21 and 22 show the Selective Color changes made to the eye area. As seen in Image 23, this one change makes a significant difference in the overall intensity of the image.

20   The quick-mask selection of the eye.

Selective Color Options

Colors: Blacks ▼

Cyan: -13 %
Magenta: +18 %
Yellow: -23 %
Black: -30 %

OK
Reset
Load...
Save...
☑ Preview

Method: ○ Relative ● Absolute

21   The Blacks Selective Color
adjustment for the eye.

Selective Color Options

Colors: Neutrals ▼

Cyan: -31 %
Magenta: 0 %
Yellow: +9 %
Black: +5 %

OK
Reset
Load...
Save...
☑ Preview

Method: ○ Relative ● Absolute

22   The Neutrals Selective Color
adjustment for the eye.

23   Before and after adjusting the eye color.

Now, here comes the fun part. Let's give this a little jolt using Zenofex Electrify filter by Alien Skin. This is a cool tool—you can really create some amazing electrical effects with this filter. I'm trying to create the effect of power pulsing thorough the subject's brain, so I used this handy filter to achieve a cool-blue electric effect applied to the motherboard layer.

Take some time to really experiment with this effect. Even the slightest of moves on the sliders can create a lot of very different effects from this sparky little filter (see Image 24).

After I applied the Electrify filter, I used the Photoshop Fade filter and faded it to 28% of its original Opacity (see Image 25). This is another awesome tool. The ability to fade and use different blending modes on an effect you have created is very powerful. In this case, it completely changes the effect and makes it blend much more seamlessly into the original image.

One last final touch I needed to add is what appears to be a light or a post to the upper-left end of the eyebrow and the inside corner of the left eye. I just used my Elliptical Marquee tool and copied one of these posts from the motherboard. Then I pasted it in place above the motherboard layer and cleaned up the edges. Finally, I transformed it to a slightly different angle to give the appearance of a post protruding from the eyebrow (see Image 26). I repeated the same process to create the post in the inner corner of the eye.

As you can see in Image 27, the change between the before and after of this image is quite dramatic. In this case, all of these effects were created more on the digital imaging than photographic side of the project. You could have produced this image by having a prosthetic piece made, placing it on to the model, and changing his skin tone with makeup and lighting. In this case, however, Photoshop's powerful effects saved a lot of time and money.

Where We Are

Well, here we are at the end of the story. I hope that in these 200 some odd pages you have found information and inspiration that was well worth your time and money. Don't just leave me sitting on the shelf now!! Pick me up once and a while just for old-time's sake. I really do want to wish all of you the best of luck in your careers and I will be smiling a little bigger if I was of any help. If you need some advice now and then, don't forget you can catch my column in every issue of *PEI*. Until we meet again…glitter, glitter everywhere….

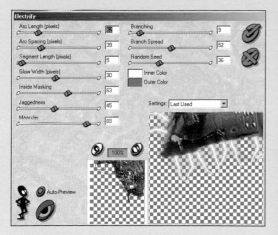

24　The settings for the Zenofex Electrify filter.

25　The Fade filter dialog box.

26　Transform box used to adjust perspective of the post.

27　Original and final images.

Index

www.informit.com

YOUR GUIDE TO IT REFERENCE

New Riders has partnered with **InformIT.com** to bring technical information to your desktop. Drawing from New Riders authors and reviewers to provide additional information on topics of interest to you, **InformIT.com** provides free, in-depth information you won't find anywhere else.

Articles

Keep your edge with thousands of free articles, in-depth features, interviews, and IT reference recommendations—all written by experts you know and trust.

Online Books

Answers in an instant from **InformIT Online Books'** 600+ fully searchable online books.

POWERED BY
Safari

Catalog

Review online sample chapters, author biographies, and customer rankings and choose exactly the right book from a selection of over 5,000 titles.

www.newriders.com

VOICES THAT MATTER

HOW TO CONTACT US

VISIT OUR WEB SITE

WWW.NEWRIDERS.COM

On our Web site you'll find information about our other books, authors, tables of contents, indexes, and book errata. You will also find information about book registration and how to purchase our books.

EMAIL US

Contact us at this address: **nrfeedback@newriders.com**

- If you have comments or questions about this book
- To report errors that you have found in this book
- If you have a book proposal to submit or are interested in writing for New Riders
- If you would like to have an author kit sent to you
- If you are an expert in a computer topic or technology and are interested in being a technical editor who reviews manuscripts for technical accuracy

- To find a distributor in your area, please contact our international department at this address. **nrmedia@newriders.com**

- For instructors from educational institutions who want to preview New Riders books for classroom use. Email should include your name, title, school, department, address, phone number, office days/hours, text in use, and enrollment, along with your request for desk/examination copies and/or additional information.
- For members of the media who are interested in reviewing copies of New Riders books. Send your name, mailing address, and email address, along with the name of the publication or Web site you work for.

BULK PURCHASES/CORPORATE SALES

The publisher offers discounts on this book when ordered in quantity for bulk purchases and special sales. For sales within the U.S., please contact: Corporate and Government Sales (800) 382-3419 or **corpsales@pearsontechgroup.com**. Outside of the U.S., please contact: International Sales (317) 428-3341 or **international@pearsontechgroup.com**.

WRITE TO US

New Riders Publishing
800 East 96th Street, 3rd Floor
Indianapolis, IN 46240

CALL US

Toll-free (800) 571-5840. Ask for New Riders.
If outside U.S. (317) 428-3000. Ask for New Riders.

FAX US

(317) 428-3280

New Riders

WWW.NEWRIDERS.COM

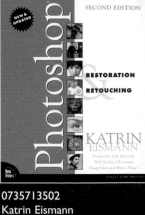
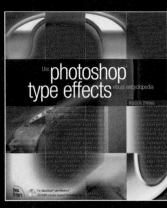

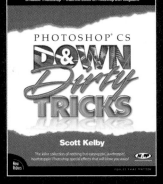
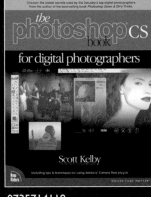

Suzette's work was produced with the help of the following fabulous companies:

Alien Skin
1111 Haynes Street, Suite 113
Raleigh, NC 27604
Toll Free in U.S.: (888) 921-SKIN
Non-U.S. Callers: 1-919-832-4124
Fax: 919.832.4065
Email: sales@alienskin.com
www.alienskin.com

Bombshell Studio Make-up
Available at Jose Eber Atelier
Beverly Hills CA
Phone: (310) 278-7646
Email: BombshellStudios@aol.com
www.bombshellstudiomakeup.com

CHIMERA Lighting
1812 Valtec Lane
Boulder, CO 80301
Phone: (303) 444-8000
Toll Free: (888) 444-1812
Fax: (303) 444-8303
Email: sales@chimeralighting.com
www.chimeralighting.com

Corel
www.corel.com

Cradoc Corp
PO Box 1310
Pt Roberts, WA 98281
Phone: (206) 842-4030
Toll Free: 1-800-679-0202
Email: info@fotobiz.net
www.fotoquote.com and
www.fotobiz.net

Dyna-Lite, Inc.
Terry Monahan
1050 Commerce Avenue
Union, NJ 07083
Corporate: (908) 687-8800
Sales: 800-722-6638
Service & Repairs: (908) 688-3210
Fax: (908) 686-6682
www.dynalite.com/

Flaming Pear
www.flamingpear.com

Fuji
www.fujifilm.com

Out West Studios
1265 South Cochran Ave.
Los Angeles, CA 90019
Phone: (323) 816-2918
Fax: (323) 933-1535
Email: steve@myronbeck.com
www.outweststudio.com

Studio B.
62 Nassau Drive
Great Neck, NY 11021
Phone: 800-Studio B
Fax: (516) 706-2369
Email: webmaster@studiob.com
www.studiob.com

Really cool people you WANT to work with:

Cynthia Bachman
Celebrity Makeup Artist
Creator of Bombshell
Studio Make-up
Phone: (818) 360-9119
www.CynthiaBachman.com

Wenceslaus Chan
Associate Creative Director VP
Grey Worldwide
777 Third Ave.
New York, NY 10017
Phone: (212) 546-2000

Judith Brewer Curtis
Costume Designer/Stylist
Phone: (310) 478-4139 or (310) 780-1876

Jeanne Fulton
VP, Senior Art Producer
Grey Worldwide
777 Third Ave.
New York, NY 10017
Email: Jfulton@grey.com

Bill Harper
Art Director
Rooftop Communications, LLC
Phone: (443) 621-0382

Thomas Herbrich
Dusseldorf, Germany
Phone: 49-211-463 260
Fax: 49-211-489 539
Email: thomas@herbrich.com
www.herbrich.com

Klaus Lucka
300 East 51st Street
New York, NY 10022
Phone/Fax: (212) 838-4338
Email: klauslucka@aol.com
www.klauslucka.com

Otto Models and Talent Agency
Tereza Otto
Phone: (323) 650-2200
www.ottomodels.com

David Rogelberg
Studio B.
Phone: 1 800 Studio B
Fax: (317) 578-2567
Email: david@studiob.com
www.studiob.com

Jeff Sedlik
Sedlik Productions
Phone: (213) 626-3323
Email: jeff@sedlik.com
www.sedlik.com

Joan Sherwood
PFI Magazine
229 Peachtree St NE, Suite 2200
International Tower
Atlanta, GA 30303
www.peimag.com

Chris Tarantino
Photoshop Consultant
Hi End Boutique Retouching
Photoshop Author
Phone: (203) 877-1507
Email:
christopheredmund@mac.com

Jerome Andrew Terry
Hairstylist to the Rockstars
Allen Edwards Salon; Encino, CA
(818) 981-7711
Lukaro Salon; Beverly Hills, CA
(310) 275-2536

Colophon

The glitterguru on Photoshop: From Concept to Cool was laid out and produced with the help of Microsoft Word, Adobe Acrobat, Adobe Photoshop, Adobe Illustrator, and QuarkXPress on a variety of systems, including a Macintosh G4. With the exception of pages that were printed out for proofreading, all files—text, images, and project files—were transferred via email or ftp and edited onscreen.

All body text was set in the font Sabon. Figure captions and notes were set in the font Tekton. The chapter headings on the opener pages were set in the font French Roast; chapter opener text and running footers were set in the font Spumoni. Headings within each chapter were set in the fonts Postino and MetaPlus. The Symbol and Zapf Dingbats typefaces were used throughout for special symbols and bullets.

The glitterguru on Photoshop: From Concept to Cool was printed on 70# Influence matte at R.R. Donnelley and Sons, Roanoke, VA. Prepress consisted of PostScript computer-to-computer technology (filmless process). The cover was printed on 12pt C2S at Moore Langen, Terre Haute, IN.

Chapter Opening Art

Kathy Griffin for "The Late Late Show with Craig Kilborn"
(Chapter 1)

Client: Hewlett Packard
(Chapter 2)

"Sacred Cow"
(Chapter 3)

Client: Bombshell Studio Make-up
(Chapter 4)

Client: Bombshell Studio Make-up
(Chapter 5)

"Alexa"
(Chapter 6)

PEI Magazine, "Digital Statuette"
(Chapter 7)

"America the Beautiful"
(Chapter 8)

"The Borg"
(Chapter 9)